Society's Breakthrough!
Releasing Essential Wisdom and Virtue in All the People

Jim Rough

Author's note

Since writing **Society's Breakthrough**, the Center for Wise Democracy (www.WiseDemocracy.org) has sparked many experiments with the central idea of the book. The "Wisdom Council Process" works. That is, the seemingly fantastical benefits are realistic and accessible, even without the suggested Amendment to the Constitution.

Jim Rough   11/30/11

ISBN: 0-7596-9168-1

Library of Congress Control Number: 2002090422

This book is printed on acid free paper.

Printed in the United States of America
Bloomington, IN

www.SocietysBreakthrough.com

1st Books - rev. 04/17/02

Dedication

To the Founders of the United States of America, who sparked a society-wide Breakthrough that deeply affects all of us today . . . and who also, unknowingly, gave us the key to society's next Breakthrough.

Contents

Part I

TRANSCENDING THE GAME

We need a new conceptualization of our problems and a revised understanding of what it will take to eradicate them. We must fundamentally change the way we think.

Marianne Williamson, *The Healing of America*

— 1 —

Society's Breakthrough! Overview

All truth passes through three stages. First, it is ridiculed. Second, it is violently opposed. Third, it is accepted as being self-evident.

Arthur Schopenhauer

What is fundamentally the most significant problem we face as a society? For a number of years I have been asking this question and have appreciated the deep conversations that quickly develop. People believe we have become materialistic, alienated from one another, disempowered, depersonalized, and caught up in making a living—diminished in some way. Concern is expressed about the unfair distribution of wealth, the loss of community and citizen involvement, the impending collapse of the environment, our increasing bureaucracy, and the general lack of good sense in our collective actions. All of the comments suggest a breakdown in our underlying system—the way we have structured and organized ourselves economically, politically, and socially.

This book explains why this breakdown is occurring and proposes a specific remedy—a capital "B" Breakthrough. It shows how we can subtly adjust the system to help us make a giant leap forward on all these issues simultaneously.

That's what a Breakthrough is—a simple change that makes a huge difference. True Breakthroughs challenge the paradigm of our times, the set of assumptions that circumscribe our lives. Even if no outward risk can be found, a Breakthrough is felt to be threatening until the paradigm shifts. Once that happens, the idea seems like common sense, only it's a new common sense.

Limits to Our Current System

To illustrate how one little change might transform many difficult, seemingly impossible-to-solve issues, consider the old story of the three blind men who encounter an elephant. One finds a leg and says that an elephant is like a tree. Another approaches from behind, touches the tail and says that an elephant is very much like a rope. The third comes to the front of the elephant, and feeling its trunk, says an elephant is like a snake.

Pretend for a minute that the elephant is restless, causing problems for each of the men. The tree-like legs are stepping all over the vegetables in the garden; the rope-like tail is whipping the blind man in the face; and the snake-like trunk is destroying a nearby bush. Not understanding the whole system, each man then works hard to solve his particular problem. One tries to turn the tree-legs into posts, heaping dirt around them. Another attempts to cut off the rope-tail. The third squirts poison at the snake-trunk to protect himself. The elephant, of course, doesn't benefit from these actions, nor do the other men.

Generally, this is how we approach societal problems—as though they are separate and as though we can use methods of control to fix them. But a Breakthrough allows us to see the whole elephant and respond intelligently. With this seeing, we might place some food nearby to motivate the elephant to move to a more advantageous location for all concerned. On its own, then, the elephant itself will eliminate the separate, individually confounding issues.

However, such a simple appearing "whole system" answer might be resisted by the blind men. Even though each may care deeply about the problem he addresses and wants it solved, the narrowness of his perspective may cause him to believe the new solution is irrelevant and resist it. What value could there be, they might all exclaim, in placing a pile of hay nearby? After all, each is an expert in his field of study and all agree there is no value to this new idea.

Society's Breakthrough! suggests that we can address our societal problems through this kind of simple action by looking at the whole elephant. The particular Breakthrough suggested here arose from my work leading four-day seminars on *Dynamic Facilitation Skills*, teaching participants how to help groups address issues creatively and collaboratively. In the seminars, participants form small groups and take turns facilitating the others. Each facilitator helps his or her group choose difficult issues, like inadequate healthcare, racism, or improving education, and then helps people stay creative in addressing them. The facilitator doesn't participate in this conversation and isn't concerned about *what* the group ultimately decides. Instead, the facilitator manages *how* the group talks. He or she assures that everyone is heard and respected and that the process is creative.

Over the years, as groups have wrestled with these different problems, their many insights have flagged one ultimate cause: our system.

At first, I was embarrassed by this convergence. It seemed that no matter what issue the groups worked on, they eventually had the same perception—that our system is causing the problem. I thought maybe something was wrong with how I was teaching. But as more groups reached this conclusion the point sank in as being true.

Our system should facilitate us to become all we can be. It should help us make collective decisions that are wise, that work for everyone—for all species and for the planet. Currently, our system relies on competition to do this. It encourages us to excel by out-performing others, and that through this game-like process, collective decisions will be made that are best for everyone.

In the realm of politics, for instance, we have majority rule, or even plurality rule. It is a battle of pre-formed ideas and candidates with set positions. This does not set up a forum for looking deeply into issues to understand them and to determine what is best for all. Rather, it encourages candidates to seek enough votes to get their way or, failing that, to aim for compromise solutions that are "good enough." This approach guarantees arguments, shallow discussions, and a disenfranchised minority.

In economics, we also rely on competition. Our capitalist system assumes a level playing field where the best can rise to the top. It assumes that the market will generate investment, production, and distribution decisions that benefit everyone.

But times have changed. Our system no longer works as well as it once did. We are not the collection of independent farmers, fishermen, and craftspeople we once were, and for which our system was designed. And we no longer live and work in a world of infinite resources.

A competitive, game-like system assumes independent players and doesn't work if we are *inter*dependent. That is, the more we resemble one organism, one elephant, the less we benefit from competition. When competition predominates within an organism, like between the heart and lungs for blood, then the organism dies.

The focus of this book is to describe a simple adjustment to our system, without really changing it, that would facilitate us out of this dependence on competition. It would help us individually and collectively to become more conscious, more trusting and better at thinking through issues.

Our System

What is our system? Where did it come from? How did it gain control?

The answer to these questions came to me as an epiphany in one of the small groups of my seminars: The U.S. Constitution is our system. It is probably the greatest social innovation in history, having sparked a shift away from tyranny toward liberty and justice for most of the world's people. But it is also the primary cause for society's big problems.

At the time, I didn't know how this could be, or see anything particularly wrong with the Constitution. But the insight pushed me to look at it deeply. How could the U.S. Constitution, for instance, have anything to do with today's international terrorist threats or with the environmental crisis?

I discovered a problem, not with the design of the Constitution, but with how this design has supplanted the functioning of We the People. No design can be left in charge of itself and us forever. The problem is that because of the Constitution, you and I have abdicated our responsibility for the system we are in. We face big problems, but there is no "we" to address them.

The question for me then became: Is there a way, with one amendment to the Constitution, for We the People to reassert control over our system? Is there a way that we might come together and seek what is best for all, rather than automatically relying on self-interested competition? And can we do this with little or no risk?

Yes! We can. There is a simple answer to this "elephantal" question that I call the "Citizens Amendment to the U.S. Constitution." Enacting it would transform how we think and act, both individually and collectively. It is like placing hay near the elephant, a win/win strategy for solving most of the really big problems in society.

The Nature of a Breakthrough

Once I "got" that the Amendment would work, I thought people would listen excitedly when I described it to them. I flew to Washington D.C. half expecting someone in power to say, "Great idea! I wonder why we didn't think of that before. We'll get to work on it right away." That didn't happen.

The normal response to a Breakthrough is not excitement over new possibilities, but rapid dismissal. It is seen to be irrelevant and concerns predominate the subsequent discussion. But these concerns are not with the idea itself, that it poses some risk, for instance. The concerns are that the immense benefits which are claimed might not be so large, or that the idea might be difficult to implement. And even when these minor concerns are readily addressed, it's still as though a fatal flaw has been found.

It is natural for people to respond to a Breakthrough critically at first. Such an idea requires some kind of inner shift for people to "get" it. A friend experienced this shift in a dream. She had been reading this book and making notes that reflected her concerns and questions. That night she had a dream where she saw herself asleep for a long time. Then she rose and joined people in the streets, feeling joy at being alive. After the dream, her concerns and questions melted away, as she found herself excited about the idea, wondering why others she talked with didn't see its merit as she did.

One example of a societal Breakthrough has helped me understand how this shift works. In Europe during the 1840's, childbed fever was killing as many as one-third of all women who delivered babies in hospitals. At that time, doctors would go straight from examining cadavers in the morgue to the delivery room, wiping their hands on their smocks. Dr. Ignatz Semmelweis had been working on this problem for many years and discovered that the deaths could be eliminated if doctors simply washed their hands in a disinfectant solution before touching pregnant women. After testing his hypothesis and proving it worked, he published the data and waited for the new practice to be embraced.

But important doctors had proclaimed authoritatively that childbed fever was the result of bad air, bad blood, sin, diets, moods, and other causes. Respect for authority was at issue here, and Dr. Semmelweis was a country bumpkin compared to these distinguished doctors. For them to wash their hands in chlorinated lime every time they touched a patient would have undermined their authority and threatened their relationship with patients. Even though Dr. Semmelweis could demonstrate that his idea worked to save lives and he presented the confirming data, it threatened the authority-based paradigm of those times. Emotional resistance prevailed.

These doctors resisted Dr. Semmelweis's Breakthrough, even though it meant losing patient lives, and possibly even the lives of close relatives, because acting on the idea meant challenging the basis of existing society. It meant seeing an elephant that wasn't supposed to be there. For the medical establishment to begin acting on Dr. Semmelweis's discovery, Dr. Louis Pasteur needed to first demonstrate that germs carried disease, and Joseph Lister needed to show how antiseptics could kill them. Only after disease could be visualized in this way did the imperative of washing hands become obvious, the new common sense. Once the elephant was seen, many other cures far beyond childbed fever could also be discovered, like reducing the 90 percent death rate from amputations, protecting against infections in general, and aiding with maladies such as food poisoning and syphilis.

The Citizens Amendment

The U.S. Constitution was a societal Breakthrough in its time. It established a new and revolutionary basis for society—the idea that a set of agreements can be in charge rather than the whims of one person. It put this concept into practice in a way that was a great leap forward for humankind.

Now, I suggest that another leap forward is to recognize the elephant that has arisen from our dependence on these agreements. The real basis for society must always be a *living conversation*. The Citizens Amendment to the U.S. Constitution, while leaving the agreements alone, helps us to acknowledge the importance of this conversation and to shape positively. It is summarized below:

> *Each year twenty-four registered voters will be randomly selected in a lottery to form a Citizens Wisdom Council. This Wisdom Council will be a symbol of the people of the United States. It will meet for one week to choose issues, talk about them, and determine consensus statements. To ensure creative conversation and unanimous conclusions, the meetings are aided by a facilitator. At the end of the week, the Wisdom Council will present the statements to the nation in a new ceremony, from "We the People" to the people. The Citizens Wisdom Council will then disband permanently and the next year a new Wisdom Council will be randomly selected.*

That's it. There's little risk. There is no coercion. Congress, corporations, the Supreme Court, laws, the media, government programs, elections, lobbyists, and all of what our system has come to be, remain unchanged. This is simply an annual series of small groups that meet, present statements, and then disband.

It is *not* primarily an effort to influence Congress for new laws. Congress may make better laws as a result, but that is not the point. The Amendment essentially establishes an annual constitutional convention with *all* of us as delegates. It creates a way by which We the People can establish an ongoing, national dialogue, talk about how things are going, and articulate our conclusions. To the extent that We the People speak with one voice, change can happen voluntarily without laws. As you continue reading, you will see why this Amendment will come to be so powerful despite the fact that Wisdom Council statements are not binding in any way.

Today we talk as though we already live in a democracy. But this is because recent generations have redefined and watered down the term. Actually, the word "democracy" comes from the Greek "demos" which means "the common people," and "kratia" which means "power." It is where the common people have not just a vote——but real power. This is certainly not what is happening in America today. Nor did the Founders intend to create a democracy. They thought of democracy as a kind of mob rule that was sure to fail and sought to avoid it. They wanted a republic. This word comes from the Latin "res publicus," or "*thing* of the people," that is, a management system to which the people consent.

We do not live in a democracy, but democracy is the cure for what ails us. We need a way for the average person to become truly involved in facing, thinking about, and deciding the key issues. This is what the Citizens Amendment will provide. It doesn't change anything in the system as established by the Founders, but it adds a bit to facilitate "We the People" to take charge of that system.

Those selected for Wisdom Councils could be anybody. They would be placed in a situation far different from what congressional representatives experience. They would have no constituency. They could speak their minds and hearts, and change their views without repercussions. They would have no predetermined topics to discuss, no special interests to represent, and no coercive powers to exert. The Wisdom Council is designed for a higher quality of conversation than elected representatives can achieve, one beyond debate and argument.

"But how can any group not argue? And how can they be expected to reach unanimous views on difficult issues?" you may ask. Actually, it's easy. It only seems difficult because our experience is rooted in the current structure, which is designed for battling. I once demonstrated this for an audience by asking them to choose a contentious issue that I would facilitate for 30 minutes. The group picked the abortion issue.

First, the usual pro-life and pro-choice positions were expressed. Our current system is structured for a discussion between these two positions. I captured them on flip charts as two possible solutions without trying to define the problem. Then I asked for more possible solutions. There was a period of silence because it seemed as if these two were the only possibilities. Finally someone broke the silence and asked a question. "How frequent are abortions anyway?" Then the group wondered if there wasn't some way to eliminate abortions altogether. At the end of the 30 minutes, this new perspective became the group's consensus. It wasn't a consensus on one of the two obvious choices, pro-life or pro-choice, but an agreement on a definition of the problem: "How can we achieve a society where all children are conceived and born into families that want and love them?"

This kind of consensus, a pulling together of what everyone thinks, *can always be reached.* Our current system doesn't encourage it, but the Wisdom Council does. Those in a Wisdom Council need not restrict themselves to one definition of the problem or some limited set of possible answers. In this setting of people, the consensus might be a problem-statement or a shared vision. They engage in a kind of talking and thinking that brings people together rather than tearing them apart. In later chapters, I'll go into more graphic detail about this and how it will affect the larger society.

Your Response

At this point, if you are thinking, "These claims are too much. What real difference would this amendment make? Twenty-four is too small of a group. How can a diverse group of people reach consensus? Who will control the facilitator? It might be a good idea, but why does it need to be an amendment? This has no chance of happening," you are not alone.

Many of us are beginning to realize that our current system isn't working. Dee Hock, founder of VISA, International, says in his book, *Birth of the Chaordic Age*, "We are experiencing a global epidemic of institutional failure that knows no bounds. We must seriously question the concepts underlying the current structures of organization and whether they are suitable to the management of accelerating societal and environmental problems—and even beyond that, we must seriously consider whether they are the primary cause of those problems . . ."

Within our system, we can elect better leaders and promote better laws and programs. But these actions can't address the underlying system, our way of thinking. Most legislation gets compromised before it becomes law anyway.

Or we can focus on education and on raising the consciousness of people. But this isn't going to make the needed difference either, because we are dealing with a living system, more than with a collection of people. We must address the whole elephant as well as the individual pieces. Because the Citizens Amendment is unique in its ability to address the elephant, we can rapidly affect all issues and all people at once.

Remember the question that started this book? Take a moment to answer it before proceeding.

What is fundamentally the most significant problem we face as a society?
Your answer:

_____

_____

Whatever you answer, to the extent that you *care* about solving it, and to the extent that it currently seems *unsolvable* to you, then you have identified a crisis in our society. It is when we are in crisis that we are most open to new ideas and to change. So, just caring about this issue and holding this crisis in mind can help you read this book. Whatever problem you name, I think you will find that the Citizens Amendment will provide a Breakthrough to solving it.

Getting Started

Most books that tackle deep societal issues focus primarily on understanding and defining the problem, maybe ending with a chapter or two on potential solutions. But this book does the opposite. Except for *Chapter 3 — The Problem: We Are Caught in the Game,* the chapters of this book basically describe different perspectives of how and why the Citizens Amendment would work.

You will agree, I'm sure, that unnecessary changes should not be made to the Constitution. This document is to be honored and protected for what it has enabled us to do and become. But at the same time, our situation is changing and We the People are ultimately responsible for the actions of our system, including its effect on us. We must not abandon that responsibility.

Thomas Jefferson raised this same point in a letter he wrote to his friend, James Madison, on September 6, 1789. From the actuarial tables of his time, he had calculated that a majority of any given generation would be dead after about nineteen years. With this statistic in mind, he wrote: "It may be proved that no society can make a perpetual constitution, or even a perpetual law. The earth belongs always to the living generation. . . . Every constitution, then, and every law naturally expires at the end of 19 years. If it be enforced longer, it is an act of force and not of right."

He speaks an obvious truth. Because we ignore it, We the People of today are governed by a system we did not consent to, that was not designed for our times, that assumes the worst in us, and that has set us on an unsustainable path. Furthermore, we have been left by this system with a very small role to play in setting things right. We the People of today need to get ourselves back into the action and take charge. We need to do it safely, with little risk. The change proposed here is a way for us to do that.

− 2 −

The Founding of True Democracy

The question is, will we cling fanatically to our decaying way of life and outmoded ideas or help the phoenix rise from the ashes?

William Ophuls, *Requiem for Modern Politics*

*I*n the science fiction movie, *The Matrix*, the protagonist discovers that life as we know it is actually a computer generated illusion. He discovers that all of us unknowingly live *virtual* lives—going to work, taking vacations, and raising families inside a computer generated reality that is projected onto our minds by a machine in the twenty-second century. If this were true, all of society's problems could easily and simply be solved through a slight programming adjustment to that machine.

In a sense it is true. But the virtual reality we share does not arise from a machine in the twenty-second century like the story of the movie. The computer that projects our reality is in the eighteenth century. It is the U.S. Constitution. It projects a "reality" that determines many of our attitudes, how we think, and even decisions we make. Collectively, for example, the U.S. Constitution orients us more toward competition than collaboration, debate instead of dialogue, judgment rather than creativity. It aims to control behaviors through laws rather than to facilitate people toward shared values. But with the addition of the Citizens Amendment, the U.S. Constitution would project a different reality. With it we would become more collaborative than competitive, more thoughtful than argumentative, and we would exercise our creativity in the service of all.

Let me give an illustration of how a small, simple addition to the structure of something can change our thinking. Consider the effect of the word "please" added to a sentence. Although technically it adds no new information, it can change the entire atmosphere and meaning of an interaction. If you say to your fifteen-year-old daughter, "Clean up your room!" you project a reality where you are trying to manage her behavior through a command. If a conversation arises, it will be a yes/no discussion, a power struggle. You and she will go back and forth about cleaning the room, arguing who is in charge. The final result will either be "yes," "no," or some compromise in between.

But just by adding the phrase, "would you please," with an appropriate attitude, you project a different reality. You are still letting her know what you want, and she still may or may not comply, but this time you are not projecting control. You are respecting your daughter's autonomy and accepting that the ultimate choice is hers. Whether she cleans her room or not is less important in this case than your relationship of respect for one another.

With the addition of "please," you may learn more about each other. You may build your relationship, discover new options, and at the same time, both of you will grow as people. For instance, your daughter may become more sensitive to your needs. That's creating a new option. Or, you may become less concerned about what she does in her room. This is yet another option. Or, you may design a new strategy that works for both of you. Adding the word "please" doesn't change *what* is being said, just *how* it is said. It changes the *dynamic* of thinking and talking.

Adding the Citizens Amendment to the Constitution is a similar reprogramming. It, too, changes the dynamic of thinking and talking, orienting us away from power and control, toward respect and creativity.

Three Structures/Three Cultures

There are basically three ways to organize a large society. I've termed them the Triangle, Box, and Circle. The Triangle structure is authority-based, with a king, father, or some "Great Leader" making the ultimate decisions. The Box system is contract-based, with everyone agreeing to abide by a document, a set of rules, or agreements. The Circle system is dialogue-based, where the ultimate decisions arise from what I term a *Choice-creating* conversation.

There is a natural progression among these three systems—from dependence to independence to interdependence. For example, the Triangle system corresponds to the way young children relate to their parents. They are dependent on them and the parent makes most of the decisions. The child looks to the parent as being all-knowing and all-powerful. Later, in adolescence, there is more of a need to separate from the parents. Teens are provided with a range of choices and a measure of independence, corresponding to the Box system. As long as they stay inside the rules, they are free to do what they want. But basically, they are still under parental control. In adulthood, however, the parents are no longer in charge. Adults have freedom and responsibility. This represents the Circle system.

Our society is traveling along this developmental path. We took the crucial step from the authority-based Triangle structure to the contract-based Box structure when we enacted the U.S. Constitution. Now, we have outgrown our contract-based system. While we continue to manage ourselves through the Constitution, we no longer

Three Ways of Organizing

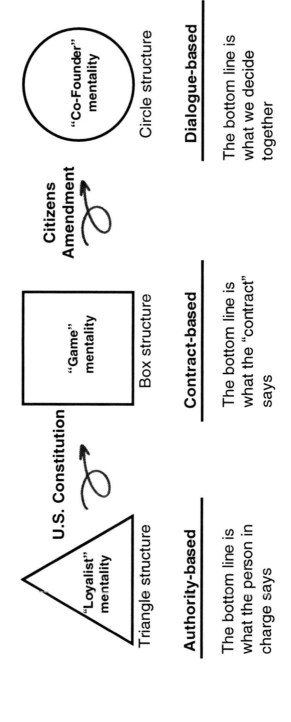

Chart #1

believe that anyone else, or their assumptions about us, should ultimately be in charge. We're ready for the Circle approach. Let me illustrate with a story about a friend of mine.

My friend lives in an intentional community. The man who organized it owned some land and found five families that were interested in living together. He gathered them so they could meet one another and examine the available lots.

To determine who would have which lot, someone in authority could have made the decision. This is the Triangle approach by which most societies have been organized. The man who owned the land could have simply appointed people to their lots. Or, in the Box approach, families could have decided ahead of time on a particular decision-making process—a lottery, pricing scheme, or vote. This would require that all stay committed to the agreement, no matter what results or situations eventually emerged.

But the families wanted something more. So they followed a third path, the Circle approach. Everyone met, talked about the lots, and sought to determine what was best for each family. Gradually over the course of a few meetings, the families grew to understand more about each other, the land, and what each one wanted and needed. Preferences changed and an overall design evolved that was endorsed by everyone.

They reached their decision through Choice-creating, an open-minded and open-hearted process where everyone seeks new options until a result occurs about which everyone feels good. While the distinction between Choice-creating and decision-making hasn't been explored fully yet, it is important to recognize that, with Choice-creating, the quality of conversation is as important as the quality of resulting decisions. Both the Triangle and Box systems are oriented to decision-making, while the Circle system orients to Choice-creating.

My friend's community has thrived for many years now. While all the families live and work independently, they meet for dinner every Sunday night in one of the homes. During these gatherings, the adults meet to talk about issues and, although they don't use the word, their quality of conversation is Choice-creating.

Not everything is decided this way. Sometimes, one person will take the lead in an activity, an authority-based structure. They also use contract-based structures. Everyone in my friend's community, for instance, has signed a legally binding document registered with the county. It says that official decisions of the community will be made by a vote of adults. This is not how they generally operate, but it provides a back-up process that would play an important role if the community were to ever disintegrate.

If my friend's community were to live according to the Box structure, they would find it far less satisfying. There would be no need for Sunday night dinners. Everyone would remain separate, just following the rules and focusing on their own lives. Group decisions would be made through voting or some other set procedure. Eventually, in deciding issues, true feelings and creative thought would be repressed. The contract-based approach supplants relationship and trust with procedure, bureaucracy, and adherence to the letter of the law.

The successful experience of this community illustrates that at least three elements are required for a Circle structure to work: (1) people must talk regularly about the important issues facing the community; (2) the talking must be held in the spirit of Choice-creating; and (3) there must exist an official, back-up contract in case the Circle breaks down.

Let's explore the three systems of organizing more fully.

The Triangle Culture: The Old Society

The traditional way to organize society is through positions of power. Because people identify with those positions, a pope, czar, or king can manage large numbers of people. For this kind of system to work, people must maintain a certain fascination with, submission to, and loyalty to these office-holders. The Triangle system inculcates a "Loyalist" mentality in people.

Loyalists see the person in power as a "Great Leader." He or she is imagined to be more capable than others, almost superhuman, caring deeply for the people in his or her charge. It is an emotional alignment where "subjects" anticipate or automatically follow commands and orient their lives toward the leader's wishes.

In his book, *Leadership Without Easy Answers*, Ron Heifitz provides a powerful reminder of the deep roots of this attitude. He sees it in the behavior of chimpanzees—"the top male appears bigger than others while he struts and dominates center stage. Everyone else is inextricably linked to him and can hardly keep from gazing at his actions. Yet, once deposed, this male shrinks while another assumes the larger-than-life role." Dr. Heifitz considers our capacity to form these authority relationships, even today, to be fundamental to organizational life and essential for human survival.

To those in the Loyalist mentality, the solutions to all problems and the answers to all questions come through a Great Leader or his teachings. Those with this perspective place supreme value on honoring him or his relics, and saying things like "Long live the King" or "Heil Hitler." Because Great Leaders draw our attention so insistently, they disempower us. We place our own lives in their shadow. The Marquis De Custine said in his *Letters from Russia* in 1839, "The Czar, the place he inhabits, and the plans that ostensibly occupy his mind are the only subjects worth thinking about, for a thinking Russian. This imperial catechism suffices for life."

Today, this phenomenon is readily apparent in many ways. When employees of corporations talk about their top leaders you can often hear the Loyalist fascination. When fans attend to the lives of their favorite movie stars or when crowds press in on presidential contenders, the Loyalist mentality is at work. The person who is the object of this fascination can easily think he or she really is that great. However, it is not so much the person, but the Triangle structure that promulgates this adulation. It generates a culture where people define their worth in terms of how loyal they are to this Great Leader, like being a loyal "subject" of the king. Those close to him don't mix with the common folk—and vice versa.

For millennia, this way of being and of organizing was "common sense." It was only after the scientific revolution, the Enlightenment, and the invention of the printing press that it was seriously called into question. During this period, scientists were realizing their own authority and not relying on the Church or the king for answers about how nature worked. When Galileo looked through his telescope and saw for himself the moons revolving around Jupiter, he accepted his own experience over the dictates of the Church. Thus, he became a threat to the "Great Authority" of the Church and to the Triangle paradigm itself.

Such scientific discoveries, plus the growing ability of people to read and learn about them on their own, powerfully undermined the old authority structure as a basis for society. A new organizing principle was evolving, the idea that there are inviolable laws of nature that anyone can discover and that everyone, even kings, must obey. But the pivot point for swinging mainstream society to this new organizing principle was the adoption of the U.S. Constitution. This was the necessary structural adjustment to transform the Triangle culture into the Box culture.

The Box Culture: Current Society

The second way of organizing society is the Box structure, where society is run by a set of agreements or rules, rather than a person. This generates a culture and way of thinking in which people are free to do what they want within the rules. It's the "Game" mentality. Within a game, the rules must be followed and there is a way to keep score. It's as though we are all in a competition for results. People are aimed, not to follow their intrinsic motivation, where they seek to discover and follow their passion, but to be extrinsically driven, to pursue votes, status, recognition, money, promotions, grades in school, or other measurable factors. Ideally, this creates a meritocracy, where the best rise to the top.

The logic is, that if the rules are good and we compete effectively, the whole system will benefit. For example, it is assumed that governments get the best office-holders if candidates compete for the positions. But it is natural in such a system that candidates do whatever it takes to win, such as avoiding the big topics, adopting simplistic positions, talking in sound bites, and hurling criticisms at their opponents. These behaviors have been shown to work and politicians either learn to adopt them or lose. Yet these behaviors aren't the best for society.

The Box system requires blind adherence to the rules. For instance, in the extremely close presidential race between Al Gore and George W. Bush, there were allegations of voting fraud and miscounting in Florida. But the way our system works, the laws as interpreted by the courts are ultimately in charge. No one can say, "Hey, there's been some confusion so let's talk about what to do." In the Box system this would lead to chaos. We just follow the rules to see who won. To decide our important collective priorities, like allocating money among defense, heath care, and environmental research, for example, we rely on a competition among special interests, and hope things will work out for the best.

The Box structure creates a competitive marketplace that promotes the Game mentality. It teaches us to compete, to buy more stuff, to earn more money, and to focus on results instead of process. At the same time, it atomizes our thinking, telling us to not worry about the larger issues in life because, if everyone follows the rules, things will take care of themselves. So we focus on our own interests and on our material well being, even when we might really want to help others. We invest our money to make more money rather than investing in what we might want to see take form in the world. We seek to reduce our taxes, even though we might really want to donate money to society.

Another crucial dimension to the Box structure is how it is established and managed. The Box system requires someone to set it up and put it in motion. Once in motion, this manager largely leaves it alone, but uses numbers to assess how well things are going and to make slight adjustments to the rules. The Box system teaches and encourages this kind of hands-off management style, valuing a numerical assessment of progress, rather than dialogue about how things are going, and top-down adjustments to the system.

So if you have ever been elected to a school board, or placed in charge of an organization, you have felt this pressure to manage this way, through the levers of power, like rules, policies, and measures. Certainly our political system is oriented this way, as are most corporations, which manage employees through incentives, recognition, reprimand, and coercion.

In the Box structure each of us assumes both roles at times—being a player within the rules and being a manager through the rules. This structure made perfect sense to the Founders in the eighteenth century because times were simpler then and because that is how the science of the day assumed God managed the universe. It was as though God designed it to have natural laws and then let go, leaving humans free within those constraints.

In the past there was a great deal of consistency and workability to this approach, but now it isn't working so well. The meritocracy has turned into what futurist and economist Hazel Henderson calls a "mediocracy." And today's science has a different story to tell about how the universe really works. The modern story of quantum mechanics, evolutionary biology, and cosmology is more consistent with the Circle structure than the Box. Things aren't as static and measurable as we once thought. The universe evolves forward without hard and fast laws, more like a conversation than a game.

The Circle Culture: The New Society

To establish the Circle structure is to take the next developmental step. It does not mean eliminating the Game. In fact, the rules can stay the same. It's just that the Game is no longer in charge of itself and us. We the People are in charge of it.

Through the Citizens Amendment, we structure dialogue outside the boundaries of the Game, empowering people to face the big issues and to be creative in solving them. This new structural piece generates a "Co-founder" mentality, where each of us actively co-creates our system together. There is more freedom and more responsibility. The Constitution and the rule of law are still there, but with them is a larger conversation that is actually in charge.

The movie, *The Legend of Bagger Vance*, illustrates this. A local boy is playing in an exhibition match against the two best golfers in the nation. Near the end he gains on the other two until he is only one stroke behind. Then our hero, while getting ready for a shot, removes an obstruction next to his ball, causing it to roll an inch. Technically, even though he gained no advantage from it, the rules say he must take a penalty of one stroke.

In the story, neither his competitors, nor anyone in the crowd, wants him to take the penalty. And certainly he doesn't want to. They invite him to say that the ball merely rolled in place and didn't move. But he declares that it did move and takes the penalty. The point is that the players and townspeople begin a larger conversation that transcends the rules of the game. They momentarily create a Circle system where people reach consensus on what should happen. But in the end, our hero chooses to adhere to the rules of the game anyway. With the Citizens Amendment in the Constitution, a similar national conversation is established where we would take ownership of the rules. With this in place, like the hero of the movie, we follow them not because we have to, but because it is right. We become empowered within our system to be "Co-founders," with authority over the system of rules.

The Co-founder mentality is demonstrated by a statement from the People's Earth Declaration (from the International Forum in Rio de Janeiro in 1992): "We wish to remind the world's political and corporate leaders that the authority of the state and the powers of the private corporation are grants extended to these institutions by the sovereign people. It is the people's right that governments and corporations remain accountable to the public will and interest." This empowered viewpoint is how all of us should feel about our system. We created it and we granted these powers to various institutions.

Currently, this statement is hollow because there is no "we" to back it up. It is just a statement by a few in the name of all of what should be true. To make this statement true, We the People must become a real force.

To illustrate the difference between the Game attitude and the Co-founder attitude, I often ask audiences, "How many of you believe people should obey the law?" All hands go up. Then I ask, "How many of you believe people should ALWAYS obey the law?" I'm still waiting for someone to raise a hand. Of course, we should obey and enforce laws. But in the Circle system neither laws nor the Constitution are the *ultimate* source of right and wrong. In the end, we must look inside ourselves to know what is right.

After World War II, the world publicly recognized this truth in Nuremberg, Germany. There were no international laws by which to hold Nazi leaders accountable for their attempt at genocide. In fact, their defense was that they were following the laws of their country. Nevertheless, the people of the world were revolted by these clearly wrongful acts, and put them on trial anyway for "crimes against humanity." The crime of the Nazis, in other words, was that they didn't look within themselves to find the clear and deep knowing of right and wrong that we all share.

With the Co-founder mentality, each of us relies less on *extrinsic* standards and measures. We look deeply inside to determine what is right and to know what to do. Paradoxically, the result of this thoughtful, inner questioning is not increased selfishness or lawlessness, but the discovery of innate wisdom, virtue, and the motivation to serve others. In a quiet moment of reflection away from the Game, people find that what really drives them, what they really want in life, is to help others and to serve life.

The crucial ingredient in the Circle system is a Choice-creating dialogue, involving everyone, that supports all to find this inner wisdom and virtue. When we engage with others about difficult issues and stay creative, we experience our uniqueness and connectedness. It's a paradoxical combination of both increased autonomy and coherence with others.

The Circle Is the Solution

Because the proposed change is a Constitutional amendment, people often assume it is primarily intended to influence legislation or government. Although it will certainly affect legislation, this effect is minor in comparison to its overall effects on people and systems. Actually, it is a change to reality itself because it adjusts the eighteenth century computer that defines our reality. With it, you and I will see things differently and act differently. See Chart #2.

The reality-changing, system-changing effects of the Amendment will open new doors for progress on many issues. Interestingly, it may be that the most effective strategy for us to solve local issues, sometimes even personal issues, is to enact this amendment to the U.S. Constitution.

As an example, let's take a look at improving your local school. The most direct way, of course, is to assure that there are good

Structure Affects Culture

LOYALIST CULTURE

- Look to the leader for direction and right answers.

- Government is in charge. Be loyal and don't challenge authority.

GAMESMAN CULTURE

- You are free within the rules. Success is up to you.

- Government is "them" not "us." They make the rules and get out off the way.

CO-FOUNDER CULTURE

- Work with others to figure out what is best for all.

- Government is "us" not "them." We the People provide the leadership.

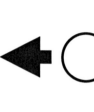

Triangle structure

Box structure

Circle structure

We the People

Chart #2

teachers in the classroom, that there are proper facilities and programs, and capable administrators. These are certainly important. But many schools already have these and more, and are still experiencing problems. They have bored kids, increased violence, poor test results, failed levies, burned out teachers, etc. School improvement programs appear one after the other to solve these problems, arriving with fanfare, then quickly losing steam and being discarded. What's going on?

The real problem is the overall system within which schools operate. The key to effective education is releasing the natural enthusiasm for learning in students and for teaching in teachers. When people are genuinely interested in the topics of study and they can facilitate the growth of one another, real learning happens. The Box system restricts this.

In the Box system, the ultimate client is not the student's passion for learning. It's the Game. The aim is for students to gain the right kind of knowledge, that which is measurable, so they can compete in the job market. Since trust, genius, passion, creativity, motivation, and deep learning cannot be measured, the system doesn't value these as much. Worse, because of the system, when the principal, school board, and state legislature start to "fix" the problems of education, they resort to more of what is causing the problem in the first place: measures and controls, standardized tests, rewards, union contracts, discipline policies, grades, etc. The heart of the problem is the extrinsically oriented system established by the Box structure. It diminishes intrinsic motivation and many human qualities, and also lessens the possibility of excellence in learning.

The movie, *Dead Poet's Society*, is a dramatic illustration. A true educator (played by Robin Williams) comes to a boys' school and evokes passion for learning. He enlivens student enthusiasm for poetry so that his students no longer follow the prescribed curriculum. They quest after the real spirit of poetry, following the muse where it may take them. To parents and administrators rooted in the Box system, these empowering changes to the students threaten a loss of control. Naturally, they act to reestablish the top-down order of things.

The movie accurately portrays the pain that students feel when control is re-imposed on our creativity and passion. One student cannot bear the thought of returning to his inside-the-box existence and commits suicide. The facilitative teacher is blamed, because if he hadn't awakened the passion, none of this would've happened. In the end, the deadening system is back in control and student creativity is muted and hidden from view.

I had a personal experience of how this feels recently while attending a class on consensus-building. As a demonstration, the teacher was managing the discussion of a controversial topic. At one point, I felt my interest in the subject rise and spoke to what was exciting me. Others in the class picked up on this and as soon as I finished speaking, many hands went up simultaneously. But the presenter saw this upsurge of energy as a threat. She reined us in because we were "getting off the topic." I felt reprimanded and found myself feeling guilt that I had not contained my excitement.

This guilt-inducing censorship of behavior is normal in the Box system. We treat passion as though it is a problem for students, teachers, and administrators. We medicate, train, counsel, manipulate, and reprimand it out of them, making problems worse. Only in a Circle culture do schools have a genuine opportunity to transform themselves. Then student genius and passion for learning will be valued more than test scores and behavior management.

In another brief example, even though the Amendment is not primarily about politics, let's consider the impact it would have on the tone of politics. Rex Weyler, co-author of the book, *Chop Wood Carry Water,* recently wrote an article, "Ten Things Wrong with Democracy," where he described the unsatisfactory ways politics now work. Because the Citizens Amendment would transform the culture and create an inclusive dialogue about what is best for all, these problems would be eliminated or reduced. The ten are:

1. *Duality* — every issue gets split into two opposing views.
2. *Misdirection* — candidates spend most of their efforts positioning themselves for reelection rather than addressing the real issues.
3. *Simplification* — both problems and solutions are simplified by politicians and media for public consumption, eroding full understanding of the real issues.
4. *Separation* — issues are handled independently so that their interdependence is lost.
5. *Dumbing down* — campaigns do not appeal to excellence or intelligence, but to fears and prejudices of voters.
6. *Tyranny of the majority* — compromise is not sought, since the majority can dictate to the minority.
7. *Negativity* — those out of power criticize those in power.
8. *Aristocracy* — the poor are disenfranchised from political power while the wealthy rule.
9. *Immediate gratification* — long-term thinking is sacrificed to the most urgent biases and desires of voters.
10. *Human myopia* — the non-human world is not considered in our decision-making.

In the Circle culture, we dialogue to make joint decisions that work for all, instead of seeking only what's best for ourselves. Issues aren't dumbed down, glossed over, simplified, or framed into dualities. They are considered in their full complexity and *breakthrough solutions* are sought. It is a new type of political thinking process that builds community.

These two brief examples—local schools and the tone of politics—hint at some of the positive potential to be gained from enacting the Amendment.

From Impossible to Possible

Many people doubt whether true democracy is really possible, let alone whether it can be achieved via a single amendment to the Constitution. Often, political commentators assure us that it isn't possible. In the book, *The End of History and the Last Man*, Francis Fukyama says, "Liberal democracy may constitute the end point of mankind's ideological evolution and the final form of human government, and as such constitute(s) the end of history." He adds, "The ideal of liberal democracy [can] not be improved upon." Michael Ledeen of the American Enterprise Institute said on C-SPAN (August 18, 1996), "Democratic capitalism is certainly the most successful social system that anybody knows of at the moment. . . . There is not going to be a solution. We're not going to have solutions. Not in this life anyway."

Mr. Ledeen also quoted Gordon Wood, a noted historian. "In a diverse, pluralistic and truly popular society like that of the United States, Americans came to understand that there could be no general will, no embodiment of the single public good because there was no democratic way of discovering that general will and prioritizing that public good."

All transformations seem impossible at first. In the eighteenth century, the establishment of a republic was seen as impossible by most people. In *The Creation of the American Republic, 1776-1787*, Gordon Wood describes why: "Politics, in other words, was still commonly viewed along a classic power spectrum that ranged from absolute power in the hands of one person on one end, to absolute power or liberty in the hands of the people at the other end. The spectrum met in full circle when, it was believed, the disorder of absolute liberty would inevitably lead to the tyranny of the dictator." The pattern of the time for how new societies formed went like this: The Great Leader of a country is overthrown by the people in the name of liberty. Chaos follows until order is regained under a new

Great Leader. In the seventeenth century, this was demonstrated clearly for Englishmen when King Charles I was overthrown in the English civil war and Oliver Cromwell took over with a different title. Other demonstrations of this cycle included the French revolution of 1789, where Louis XVI was overthrown amidst idealistic zeal and democratic writings. But from that period of chaos, Napoleon Bonaparte eventually crowned himself "emperor." In the Russian revolution of 1917, the same thing happened. The Czar was overthrown amidst utopian, democratic zeal and a new Triangle structure was established around the leader of the Communist Party.

The American experience went differently because of the Constitutional Convention. The former colonists did the impossible and invented something entirely new. When they began the Revolution, they wanted to be separate from England, but didn't necessarily want a new type of society. The key difference in their case was the convening of a big meeting to talk about it.

In 1787, the most respected leaders of the former colonies gathered for a whole summer. They debated with one another behind closed doors while Americans waited anxiously. They lived together in what was then the small town of Philadelphia, meeting in taverns and homes each night. One can imagine that much of the real work was done in these informal conversations.

The gathered leaders were thoughtful and built on their knowledge of history and on their familiarity with the experience of native Americans. At the end of their long convention, they prepared a nearly unanimous proposal and suggested that it be presented to the people in state conventions.

Then the real conversations began. Over the next two years, the ideas of the Constitution were debated and state conventions were held. Only by a narrow margin was the new Constitution adopted. Although most folk were no longer loyal to the King of England, they were still habitually drawn to the Triangle concept of the Great Leader, with George Washington the focus of this attention. But he did not play along. Instead, he helped people transfer their loyalties away from him to the U.S. Constitution itself.

This was a huge step. Yes, women, native Americans, slaves, and non-property holders were largely excluded, but it was an amazingly large step toward democracy, nonetheless. And it led to a new, entrepreneurial way of thinking throughout the world.

This shift of consciousness is our proudest contribution, an increase in individual liberty, justice, and power to the common person. Over and again we have proven our willingness to sacrifice our lives to maintain this step forward in consciousness and to promote it in the world. The Revolutionary War, World War I, World War II, the Cold War, the Gulf War, and even the War on Terrorism have all been about ensuring that this evolutionary step, from the Triangle to the Box, remains firmly in place. King George III, the Kaiser, Hitler, Stalin, Saddam Hussein, and Osama bin Ladin have all tried to maintain or re-impose the old, authority-based structure and Loyalist paradigm, but Americans and others have remained true to their commitment to this new system, the rule of law.

Yet we must not allow enthusiasm for this great leap forward to limit our continued evolution. Now it is time to accomplish the impossible once again. The key to success in this next step, as well as the last, is to convene a healthy conversation.

From Box to Circle

Even without the Citizens Amendment, a transformation to the Circle culture is already underway. The book, *The Cultural Creatives: How 50 Million People are Changing the World,* by Paul Ray and Sherry Ruth Anderson describes how, through survey instruments and interviews, the authors have discovered the emergence of a new subculture. They describe this growing collection of people as "Cultural Creatives," people who hunger for deep change "in the direction of less stress, more health, lower consumption, more spirituality, more respect for the earth and the diversity within and among the species . . ." These people are beginning to pull away from Box values and live according to Circle values on their own initiative.

The authors state that this subculture started sometime after World War II and has grown to about 50 million people. They suggest that, even though it is becoming populous, the people in it feel themselves to be alone because they have not yet figured out how to link into a coherent political force. The Box structure must change if this linkage is to happen. Without the Citizens Amendment or something like it, the Box structure will continue to enforce a mainstream Game mentality, and the Cultural Creatives will always be a backwater.

Similarly, before the Constitution was enacted, there was a growing Box subculture in Triangle times. People believed in natural laws and longed for personal liberty and the rule of law, but were not to achieve them until overthrowing the King and adopting a workable Constitution. The same is true today. We can have a supermajority of Cultural Creatives, but we still need a structure in place that supports the shift. This time the necessary structure is not a written, agreed-upon set of procedures, it is the convening of an ongoing Choice-creating conversation among all of us.

Let me give a flavor of how such a conversation can transform an organization. Many years ago, I worked in the Operations Improvement Department of Simpson Timber Company. All departments in our company were asked to develop mission statements and we prepared one like everyone else. While the other departments met for an hour or so to develop theirs, our manager, Paul Everett, called us into a three-day meeting to develop ours. Although I balked at this use of time, I was grateful later. This extended meeting not only created the necessary statement, but it also changed our system.

In the meeting, we bared our souls, trying to seek out what we all thought was needed, what we wanted from our jobs, and trying to find one statement that worked for everyone. Without knowing it, we were holding a Choice-creating meeting. Through the process, we did far more than communicate a statement of what we did. We also created a powerful community of people within the corporation. The statement we created served as a symbol of our deeply meaningful connection to one another.

Even though we worked in a top-down company, we had become a department that no longer had a boss. Instead, we were participants in an ongoing conversation that was setting strategic direction for ourselves, and in some ways, for the company, as well.

I didn't realize how much of a change the process had made on me until a few months later when, in a hectic moment, my boss wanted me to do something his way, even though I didn't agree. Because of the confidence I had gained from our meeting, I considered this as a "request" from him, and did not grant it. After all, I knew what he and I aspired to and that, on reflection, he would support me. Later, with gratitude, he did.

The Citizens Amendment invites each of us into a similar process for society. We, too, will create a shared mission, a different reality, and new symbols to empower ourselves.

— 3 —

The Problem: We Are Caught in the Game

Our current modes of rationality are not moving society forward into a better world. They are taking it further and further from that better world.

Robert Pirsig, *Zen and the Art of Motorcycle Maintenance*

*I*n the beginning of this book you were asked: *What is fundamentally the most significant problem we face as a society?* By answering, you have named an issue that deeply concerns you.

In this chapter we will look at a number of different answers to this question, seeing how each is tied to an underlying elephant—the imminent breakdown of our current system. But to consider these huge problems before appreciating how the Citizens Amendment would address them can be overwhelming or even depressing. I encourage the reader to remember that *the essence of this book is good news!*

Ten Symptoms of Society's Elephant

Below, I've taken the answers of different people and combined them into ten categories. Probably, you will recognize your issue among them. These categories are ten symptoms of the larger, elephant issue.

1. People are greedy and selfish
- People are only interested in themselves.
- People are apathetic toward the difficulties of others.
- People are materialistic and are motivated to consume.
- People see themselves as separate from nature and others.

2. People are alienated from one another.
- There is a breakdown of the family and loss of community.
- Violence and crime are becoming normal.
- Discrimination, racism, sexism, ageism, permeate our attitudes.
- There is a loss of respect for others (e.g., litigation instead of discussion).
- Taking advantage of other people (e.g., sales schemes targeted to the elderly) is considered a normal tactic for success.
- Negative media alienates people.

3. We are in a spiritual crisis.
- Disconnection from a spiritual life and from God is common.
- Drug use, smoking, gangs, alcohol abuse are the gods of choice.
- Lack of meaningful work is the lot of most of us.
- The loss of spirituality means self-destructive, addictive decisions like obesity, ill health, family deterioration, and financial difficulties.

4. Society is increasingly vulnerable.
- As individuals have greater capability to harm the community and as more people become excluded from participating in

setting society's direction, the threat of different terrorist attacks is accelerating.

- Fear of terrorism causes widespread paranoia that diminishes liberty and increases the chances of self-destruction.
- Poor decisions on the part of individuals (e.g., Enron, Chernobyl, Y2K, etc.) make angry victims of us all.
- The rapid spread of new viruses haunts us.
- New technologies (e.g., bioengineering, microwaves, and nuclear energy) are new monsters threatening us.
- Overpopulation causes or makes most problems worse.

5. *Social justice is lacking.*
   - The inequitable distribution of wealth is not only unfair but dangerous.
   - Inequitable distribution of power threatens tyranny.
   - Cycles that trap people (e.g., poverty, prison, welfare, etc.) seem unbreakable.

6. *Democracy is threatened.*
   - The influence of money on politics sells us out.
   - Increasing citizen apathy and feelings of powerlessness contribute to our paralysis.
   - Corporate dominance of the media and politics spreads complacency, misinformation, and distrust.
   - Polarization, partisanship, and politics of rage defeat our interest and involvement.
   - Alienation of citizens from their government inspires fear, distrust, and anger.

7. *Individual freedom and privacy are threatened.*
   - Burgeoning databases erode freedom and privacy.
   - Increasing government regulations cause inefficiencies and lack common sense.
   - Increasing control over our lives by large organizations turns us into automatons.

8. *Our system diminishes people.*
   - Treating people like commodities (e.g., performance standards, extrinsic motivation, and advertising) reduces our humanity to statistics and averages.
   - The rapid pace of life wears us out by forcing us to overextend.
   - The values of money and materialism promote shallowness and ignorance.
   - Loss of family, intimacy, service, or community brings feelings of loneliness and attitudes of helplessness.

9. *Collectively, we make stupid decisions.*
   - Solving symptoms instead of problems has been our normal course of action.
   - Reactive, sound-bite legislation instead of well-researched solutions is now taken for granted.
   - Elected officials cater to special interests rather than the well being of all.
   - Our inability to make societal investments (e.g., on education or the infrastructure) cripples us.
   - Encouraging economic growth rather than quality of life is bringing us closer to the precipice.

10. *Our common resources are threatened.*
   - Impending and actual environmental disasters (e.g., ozone depletion, global warming, species extinction, etc.) compound all other problems.
   - The assault on the web of trust we all share causes us to lose that trust.
   - The indiscriminate use of antibiotics, pesticides, etc. weakens our health and risks the health of future generations.

When they designed the U.S. Constitution, the Founders did not have these ten issues foremost in their minds. Instead, they were aimed at preventing tyranny and ensuring individual freedoms. So they designed a system that was a "balance of powers." It was like a game played within an agreed-upon set of rules. They were aiming for a safe, fair system that left people alone, but which oriented their efforts to the mutual benefit of all.

All ten of the fundamentally significant issues listed arise from our new circumstances combined with the Game mentality that our system promotes.

Our Game Mentality

Today we are born, live, and die within a Game. As human beings we automatically find ourselves to be players inside a set of rules, with measurable ways to gauge our success. It is only natural then, to a large degree, that we assume the perspectives and values of players. The following are some game perspectives and values we are pressured to assume:

- *Self-veiling.* Players limit their attention to what is inside the game. In his book, *Finite and Infinite Games*, James Carse calls this limited seeing and feeling "self-veiling." He describes how, many times, players won't feel pain from their injuries until after the game. Or, they will focus on the goal so much that they will take extreme risks in trying to attain it.

  The game is so compelling it commands our full attention. Although players have the freedom to step off the field of play at any time, it is difficult for them to do so because of self-veiling.

- *Know the score.* Inside a game, the ultimate value is measurable. In our game culture as well, we look to measurable results as being of ultimate importance.

- *Have fun.* Games are great fun. But to focus on fun may be to limit one's experience of his or her true nature and of what is truly meaningful. In games, meaningfulness is distorted and trivialized.

- *Win! Be competitive.* Football coach Vince Lombardi's famous words were: "Winning isn't the most important thing. It's the only thing." By adopting this attitude we trivialize relationships with others.

  We may help others, but it's done with an orientation to winning—not for the joy of helping. We see others as either team members or opponents, not as just people. A big part of our strategy with opponents is defense, keeping them from scoring. In a game it's sometimes desirable to be deceptive, to use up scarce resources, and to block others from improving.

- *Improve your skills.* Winning the game requires dedication and practice. But the emphasis is on game skills only. There is no guarantee that these are useful in other areas of life.

- *Maintain a game face.* Don't let your feelings get in the way of performance and don't let your opponent know about them because it shows your weakness. So, in a game we consider it admirable to be inauthentic, to pretend nothing bothers us, for instance.

- *Be loyal to your team.* Since a game is us versus them, loyalty is a prime value. But teams are not loyal in return. They are not communities sincerely interested in you as a person. If a better player comes along, you are expendable.

- *Keep hustling.* Don't stop until the whistle blows. There is a fast pace to the game mentality. Stay active rather than engaging in quiet reflection.

- *Innovate.* Keep thinking of new ways to improve your performance. This entrepreneurial attitude leads to many benefits. But the hidden message is "don't waste time improving yourself in ways that won't achieve results on the scoreboard." So the range of innovation is limited.

- *Obey the rules.* A focus on the rules is crucial in any game. When the players manage the game themselves, without referees, the *spirit* of the law applies. But when there is a referee, as with most of society, then the *letter* of the law applies. Then it's okay to get away with as much as you can.

- *Gain control of the rules.* When winning becomes the ultimate value, then it becomes important for you as a player to shape the rules in your favor. It is easier to win this way than by competing at someone else's game.

Of course, each of us is far deeper and richer than this set of values. But our system imposes this perspective in the same way that people in the Middle Ages knew their place in life and acquiesced to the authority of the king. These values are so much a part of life that we confuse them for human nature and think that's the way people are. But it's not. Put people inside a different structure and they demonstrate different values.

For me, an image of how this works is to picture myself sitting on the edge of my bed, getting dressed to play basketball. In that moment, I am in Real Life, acting from a desire to have fun with the guys. But once I arrive at the gym, join a team, and begin playing, everything changes. I become self-veiled and directed toward winning. Naturally, I take full advantage of the rules—going right to the edge of the boundaries of play, for example. If you were watching and didn't realize I was playing a game, you would be critical at how self-interested I was. But it's okay—it's only a game. In our basketball games, however, each player was firmly anchored to Real Life. If someone got hurt, we called "time out" and put aside the competition. We forgot about who was winning or losing in that moment and became concerned about the injured player.

Unfortunately today—collectively for sure, and also individually in some cases—we don't have a Real Life. We only know ourselves as players. Particular people might "drop out" and "get a life," but most of us are still competing, getting our cues from the commercial media that grounds our "reality."

In a way, we have become like the soccer fans that went to a match in Bradford, England, in 1985. They became so caught up in the game they ignored a fire that had started in the stands. Fifty-three fans died largely because they were unable to let go of the game and reconnect to Real Life.

In a contrasting example, Lawrence Lemieux had piloted his Finn-class boat to second position in a race at the Seoul Olympics. He was close to winning a medal, but saw another boat in trouble. A sailor from Singapore had been swept overboard. Lemieux gave up the race and rescued the man. No one was present to acclaim this act, but in this moment of crisis, he was able to realize what was truly important and escape from Game values to act on Real Life values.

It's tough to act on the values of Real Life in our system. On a PBS broadcast of *Frontline* entitled "Washington's Other Scandal" (10/6/98), Harold Ickes, former campaign manager for President Clinton, was asked how he felt about the effects of corporate campaign contributions on elections. He said, "I think the campaign finance situation in this country is in disarray, and a disgrace, and a mess. I would be the first to concede that." Then he continued with new enthusiasm, "But the question is, 'Did we purposely violate the law?' The answer is, I think, 'No.' I'm confident of that. We proceeded with lawyers at every turn." On one hand, he didn't like what the Game forced him to do, but on the other, he wanted to win and was pursuing every possible avenue.

Another example was when Bob Dole was Senate majority leader. A newsman asked him why the president and Congress have a tough time working together. His reply was blunt and honest. He said, "The opposition leader wants to make sure the President is not reelected."

In other words, unless there is some overwhelming crisis, politics is a competition that must be won.

In his book, *The Politics of Meaning*, Michael Lerner describes what this perspective eventually does to us. "We see around us the destructive consequences of the dominant ethos of selfishness and materialism. People treat one another as objects to be manipulated rather than as beings who have a fundamental worth that ought to be respected and even cherished. Many of our cultural and economic institutions teach us to look at the world from a narrow, results-oriented, materialist perspective. In the process we lose touch with the awe and wonder we experienced as children at the grandeur of the universe."

Daniel Yankelovich points out the strangeness of our approach in a *National Civic Review* article (Fall-Winter 1994). "Throughout history, most societies have placed the welfare of the group before that of the individual. American society took another path—until now, a highly successful one. We have built a viable, dynamic society by elevating individuals above the group." He adds, "It now is becoming clear, however, that this priority worked as well as it did because it was accompanied by such a strong sense of individual responsibility."

The Game is Breaking Down

Advances in technology, the industrial revolution, roads, telephones, the division of labor, the Internet, cell phones, television, just-in-time production methods, global trade, and the limits of planetary resources all connect us to one another whether we like it or not. These changes turn us into a system instead of an aggregation of individuals. They not only make us more dependent on one another, but more vulnerable as well. We become more like one entity that lives or dies as a whole. With this kind of system, extremely small fluctuations can reverberate to have huge ramifications. This is

Structure Affects EVERYTHING

Chart #3

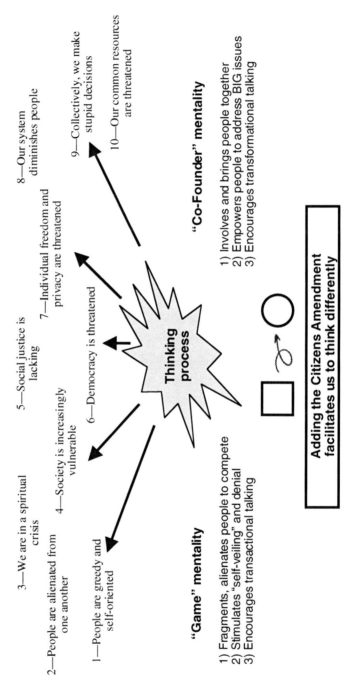

3—We are in a spiritual crisis

5—Social justice is lacking

8—Our system diminishes people

2—People are alienated from one another

4—Society is increasingly vulnerable

7—Individual freedom and privacy are threatened

9—Collectively, we make stupid decisions

1—People are greedy and self-oriented

6—Democracy is threatened

10—Our common resources are threatened

Thinking process

"Game" mentality

1) Fragments, alienates people to compete
2) Stimulates "self-veiling" and denial
3) Encourages transactional talking

"Co-Founder" mentality

1) Involves and brings people together
2) Empowers people to address BIG issues
3) Encourages transformational talking

Adding the Citizens Amendment facilitates us to think differently

commonly called the "butterfly effect," referring to how, in special circumstances, it is possible that the flick of a butterfly's wing in the Amazon basin can cause a hurricane in China.

Rushworth Kidder tells the story in *Futurist* magazine of two electrical engineers in the city of Chernobyl who, in their butterfly moment, ruined a portion of planet earth for the foreseeable future. Playing around in an unauthorized experiment at reactor #4 of the nuclear power plant there, these engineers overrode six separate computer-driven alarm systems. They padlocked valves into the open position so they wouldn't automatically close, exacerbating a design flaw in the reactor. It overheated and melted part of the core, spewing radioactive material into the air, eventually killing tens of thousands of people, and making it necessary for 167,000 people to lose their homes and leave behind the lives they knew. The engineers are dead, but the ghost city of Chernobyl remains as a permanent, toxic monument to the reality of our interconnectedness and increased vulnerability.

For our complex system to work, we must have a culture of trust, consciousness, and responsibility that everyone shares. Certainly it is important that we not exclude sub-populations from feeling this interconnectedness. It's especially important that we not alienate minorities or the "losers" of the competition. This is how terrorists are created. As Timothy McVeigh, the Oklahoma City bomber, said before he was executed for killing a hundred and nineteen people one day, " . . . isn't it kind of scary that one man could reap this kind of hell?"

Modern technology reshapes the Game to be something different than a fair competition. Robert Frank and Philip Coop, in their book, *The Winner Take All Society: Why the Few at the Top Get so Much More Than the Rest of Us,* explain how, since we can all hear the world's best opera singers, we now listen to them instead of neighborhood performers. No matter what discipline, the few at the top receive the lion's share of adulation and money, far more than whoever is in second place. They say, "As the revolution in information processing and transmission continues, there is increasing leverage for the talents of those who occupy top positions and correspondingly less room for others to find a lucrative niche."

Many situations are like this today, where there is one product, person, or performer way out ahead of everyone else, not because they are so much better, but because today's society just works that way. A chart of the distribution of wealth, for instance, shows that we've already reached a dangerous point. Currently, the world's richest person has about $70 billion, a number so large that a graph of the distribution "curve" cannot meaningfully be drawn. On a normal sized piece of paper, the "curve" is just two lines meeting at 90 degrees. For there to be any bend in the chart, where a millionaire registers as having wealth, the paper on which the chart is drawn must extend to the sky, almost beyond the atmosphere

Since money influences the media, corporations, elected officials, and even the voters, the distribution of wealth reflects the distribution of power. Those in the wealth-spike play a different Game than the rest of us, certainly different from what the Founders intended. Their Game is to turn public resources into private wealth. This is accomplished in a number of ways. If you own a baseball team, you get the voters to pay for your stadium. If you own a telecommunications company, you get Congress to give you the radio frequencies; if you are a mining company, they gift you with the mining rights to federal lands or apply lower environmental standards. It's a high stakes battle taking place outside of the limelight.

As I write this, the U.S. Congress is considering and enacting a number of new tax measures to shift the tax burden off the spike of wealthy people onto the masses, like ending the inheritance tax, reducing corporate taxes, and lowering capital gains taxes. Unbelievably, congressional representatives portray these actions as populist measures. They voted to eliminate the inheritance tax, for

The Distribution of Wealth in Society

Chart #4

A typical distribution of wealth has some curve to it.

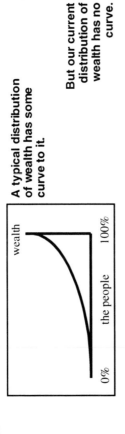

But our current distribution of wealth has no curve.

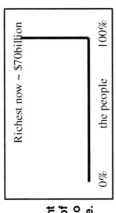

For there to be just a little curvature in our chart – e.g. where a millionaire registers one centimeter high – the chart must be extended.

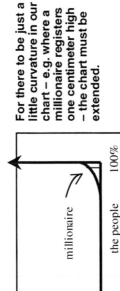

The real wealth of the bottom 60% of people has NOT increased over the past twenty years.

For every ten billion dollars owned by the richest person, the chart extends one kilometer.

example, which affects only the richest 2% of the people, by exclaiming how it protects family farms from being forcibly sold to pay estate taxes. But according to Neil Harl, Iowa State University economist, cited by *The New York Times,* April 8, 2001, there has never been an instance of a family farm being sold for this purpose.

The Rise of Corporate Power

Rich people are not to blame for the awkward distribution of wealth. It is a systems problem, largely due to the advent of the modern corporation. Originally, corporations were public entities chartered by each state for a limited time to serve specific public purposes, like building roads, bridges, or canals. After the Civil War, however, the Fourteenth Amendment was passed to ensure that no former slave could be denied the rights of citizenship. In 1886, the Supreme Court interpreted this amendment to apply to corporations as well. So, since that time, corporations have been deemed legal "persons," entitled by the Constitution to the freedoms and protections of the Bill of Rights. They have become autonomous.

Because corporations are collections of people, we think of them as driven by human values. They are comprised of good people, owned by good people and, mostly, work to provide helpful services, so we see them as corporate "citizens." But they are not like people, nor are they, in important ways, under human control. They do not eat, sleep, feel, or assume responsibility. They do not have intrinsic motivations or deep issues to resolve. Especially when owned by global capital markets instead of members of the local community, they exist solely to compete for profits in the Game.

In his book, *The Emperor's Nightingale: Restoring the Integrity of the Corporation in the Age of Shareholder Activism*, Robert Monks underscores this point. He says, "Corporations are neither people with hearts nor machines with perfect logic, but rather systems with their own dynamics, driven entities that seek unlimited life, size, power and license, eventually to the point of threatening the entire economic system with a loss of credibility—and perhaps existence."

In his book, *When Corporations Rule the World,* David Korten relates the situation to a Grade B science fiction movie: "As corporations gain in autonomous institutional power and become more detached from people and places, the human interest and the corporate interest increasingly diverge. It is almost as though we were being invaded by alien beings intent on colonizing our planet, reducing us to serfs, and then excluding as many of us as possible."

Because of corporate autonomy, the Game itself has become autonomous. It serves its own ends with no single person, corporation, or country in charge. So, for example, when Congress debated whether or not to eliminate the inheritance tax, many of the very richest people in the world argued *against* the idea. People like Bill Gates, Sr., George Soros, and Warren Buffett personally requested Congress to *not* eliminate the tax, but they did anyway. The system demanded it.

Similarly, the demands of the global marketplace are often more in charge of corporations than the owners. David Korten describes the efforts of the Haas family, who own 94% of the Levi Straus company, to be socially responsible. They cancelled $40 million a year in production contracts to protest human rights violations in China, but despite their good intentions, global market pressures forced them to close 58 plants and lay off 10,000 workers in the U.S.

Government is supposed to be in charge of all this, but, more and more, it is also controlled by the global marketplace. Even supposedly independent powers like university research labs, investigative reporters, unions, and nonprofit organizations are pressured into compliance through donations, incentives, special lobbying, legal actions, and media control.

The system is in charge of us. We live neither in a democracy, with "power to the common people," nor a republic, "a thing of the people." We live in something else altogether—a "rep-ocracy," where the "thing has the power."

As the Game gains power and increasingly determines the political agenda, regular people pull away in frustration. Any unorganized, heart-felt attempt on their part to influence legislation is easily outmaneuvered by the well-organized commercial interests of the Game. Even the richest people, elected officials, and corporate owners must eventually toe the line.

Now It's a Team Game

As employees and consumers, we can refuse to work for companies that operate immorally. We can refuse to buy their products or start our own businesses. But today the free exercise of this choice is increasingly difficult. Corporate ownership of the media, dominance of education, monopoly over jobs, and demand for products make it difficult for the average person to earn a living by standing up for what is right—or to even know what is right.

In the British anthology, *Reinventing Democracy*, Paul Hirst describes this as a creeping tyranny: "Most people have little choice but to work for large organizations and to accept services and to buy products from them. We take the power of such institutions for granted, whether it be a private company telling its employees how to dress or how often they may go to the lavatory, or a Job Club determining how many letters an unemployed person must write in a week, or some blatant piece of insolence that undermines the dignity of the consumer and is justified as 'company policy.'"

The Box system now threatens personal freedoms in other ways as well. Just through selling products and capturing markets, corporations are developing and using new databases of personal information. And as laws proliferate to try to fix this and other problems, government, too, is becoming intrusive and restrictive. Now permits are needed to replace a porch, burn trash, or start a home business. As members of a complex society that is increasingly interdependent, we are naturally subject to decisions and manipulations over which we have no say.

The advent of the corporation has changed the nature of the Game. It's now a global team Game instead of a Game played by individuals of one community. In fact, people now identify themselves more with their organization, or team, than their local community.

Team membership might seem at first glance to be the same or almost the same as community membership, because both generate strong feelings of affiliation. But the shift from community to team is actually a big change in our relationship with others. A community asks of you, "Who are you as a person?" and understands that this question can only be answered over time through experience. Certainly, it doesn't expect a quantifiable answer. A team, on the other hand, requires you to specialize. It asks you, "How well are you performing for us today?" And it wants you to provide proof through numbers.

A community is all-inclusive, committed to its members, and rooted in place. A team excludes those who don't produce results and is committed to you only as long as you perform. If not, the team moves on without you.

The team experience is still valuable. Teams are high energy, promote excellence, are efficient and focused, and they build a sense of accomplishment with others. If you are a good performer and the team does well, you are well taken care of. But they, especially corporations, ultimately serve the Game more than they serve people. It is not like Real Life where people in a community do good because it feels good. It's where people sacrifice themselves for the Game.

In her article, "The Industrial System Isn't Designed to Bring Out the Best in People," columnist Donella Meadows tells us how this self-sacrifice works: "Every day decent people clear cut forests, fish the oceans bare, spray toxins, bribe politicians, overcharge the government, take risks with the health of their workers or neighbors or customers, cheapen their products, pay people less than a living wage for a day's work and fire their friends. 'If I don't do it, my competitor will,' they say regretfully, and they're right."

Real Life values—like health, learning, meaning, love, etc.—are not inherently part of the Box system. Even for those of us who have been fortunate enough to find meaning in our work and to serve others, the Box system can still diminish us as providers along with the value we provide.

I spoke with a probation officer in a state government recently who told me how his work has changed in recent years. In the past, he had worked hard, loved his job, felt trust among fellow workers. He said that now everything is managed by performance standards. One of those standards is for him to see thirty parolees a week. "Because I must physically see them to meet my quota," he said, "I end up some weeks going around and saying 'Hi and Goodbye' to a lot of clients that don't need me and missing the opportunity to help those who do." He added, "I just don't care anymore."

His lack of caring is a new phenomenon called "burn out." People in the helping professions, like nurses and teachers, can suffer it the most. It happens when extrinsic values, like numbers and rewards, take on more importance than intrinsic values, like the joy of helping others.

I recently listened to an international group of teachers talking about how their jobs have changed. They all said that class sizes have increased and there is more pressure for measurable results. They are supposed to teach from approved curricula and the children are assessed through standardized tests. Even their relationship to the children is placed under Box control. Rules tell them not to hug a child, for instance, because the school runs the risk of a lawsuit. Students are treated as "standardized" humans instead of unique individuals.

These teachers were bemoaning how the system puts responsibility for education in the hands of the state rather than parents, teachers, and children. The crucial dialogue about what is best for children is missing, in favor of what is best for getting jobs and for serving corporations. Human qualities like love, enthusiasm, respect, wisdom, kindness, forgiveness, and consciousness are ultimately not measurable. So, the dominance of the Game, the shift from community to team, and the pretense that Real Life can be measured are diminishing to people.

The Game Makes the Decisions

Eleven years before the U.S. Constitution established a workable structure for the Box system, Adam Smith published *The Wealth of Nations* where he presented key parts of its underlying theory. He explained how a marketplace of self-interested parties can benefit all, even though this may not be anyone's direct intention. He said, "It is not from benevolence of the butcher, the brewer, or the baker that we expect our dinner, but from their regard to their own interest." In the free market system, it is as though they are "led by an invisible hand" to promote the general welfare. It is also how a game works, that just from playing, everyone has fun and grows more capable.

For the ideal marketplace to work, Smith described certain assumptions—that individual suppliers and customers must be relatively small in comparison to the market; that sellers bear the full cost of their products and pass them on in the sales price; that complete information about the products must be available; and that the rules cannot favor particular competitors. The game must be fair for all.

But, as David Korten makes clear in his book, *The Post-Corporate World: Life After Capitalism,* today's "capitalist economy directly contradict(s) the assumptions of market theory in every instance." Now, particular competitors dominate the markets they are in; industries do not include the full costs of production; the corporate-owned media distorts and restricts information; and the rules of the marketplace serve special interests rather than the general interest.

Now society's decisions serve private interests more than the public interest. Important decisions are made not to best serve all the people, but so that certain players can make a lot of money. For instance, how did we as a nation decide to emphasize automobile travel, rather than more ecologically friendly forms of transportation such as trains or buses, as was the case in Europe? In large measure, this decision came about because automobile-related industries bought up the competition, like the trolley systems in most cities, artificially managed the price of gasoline to be lower than it should, and passed on the costs of carbon dioxide emissions, global warming, the destruction of local communities, traffic jams, Middle Eastern wars, etc., to the public.

The Tragedy of the Commons

Another important way in which we are growing more interdependent and system-like is the onset of what Dr. Garret Hardin calls "the tragedy of the commons." In a brief article in *Science* magazine in 1968, he told the story of how villagers in medieval England would graze their sheep on a large common green, which belonged to everyone. As long as there was plenty of grass on the commons, villagers could add as many sheep as they were able and the additional sheep would benefit both their owner and the local economy.

As the total number of sheep grew, however, the carrying capacity of the commons was reached. At that point, the sheep were eating grass faster than it could grow. Adding more sheep meant that the grass could not regenerate itself, and the commons went into systemic decline.

Up until that point, the villagers had been able to make this decision independently, without adversely affecting their neighbors. But once the carrying capacity of the commons was reached, the actions of each villager affected all. They had become part of one system. When one villager added sheep, he received all the benefits while everyone suffered the reduced the availability of grass. For each villager as competitor, from the standpoint of short-term profits, to add sheep was the right decision because it brought the most benefit for the least cost. Likewise, the loss to the other villagers from each added sheep was small, so there was little incentive to protest. That is, the incentives of the system assured overgrazing and the long-term destruction of the commons. This actually happened many times over so that, in medieval England, "bare as a commons" became a cliche.

Dr. Hardin calls this historical pattern a "tragedy," not because of the disastrous ending, but because of the way the disaster inexorably unfolds. No one wants this end result, but because of the structure of the system, everyone is driven to make it happen. Too late, the villagers realize they are members of a finite system, and that they should have worked together.

The metaphor also illustrates how no single villager can make the necessary adjustment to save the commons. Neither can a majority of villagers. Once the carrying capacity is reached, which is our new reality, *all* must work together to assure that the commons can thrive. Without whole-system cooperation we are doomed.

In *Discovery Magazine* (9/95), Jerod Diamond describes how this tragedy played itself out on Easter Island in the Pacific Ocean. The islanders built huge stone statues in a spiritual competition seeking the favor of their gods. Building these statues sapped the resources of the island until the tragedy of the commons took hold. The tribes continued to compete until the islanders used up all higher forms of plant and animal life. Then the civilization collapsed and surviving islanders turned to cannibalism.

Today, our society has reached or exceeded the carrying capacity of many commons. The ozone layer, global forests, underground water tables, soil fertility, species diversity, and the ability of air and water to cleanse pollution are all in decline. A wide range of other tragedies is underway as well, from the growing incidence of antibiotic resistant bacteria to the fraying web of trust that sustains society. From the standpoint of the tragedy of the commons alone, we have reached the limits of our Box system and the Game mentality.

As described in the next chapter, the Citizens Amendment will solve this crucial problem by helping us make the transition from the Box system and the Game mentality, to the Circle system and the Co-founder mentality. It will give us hay for the elephant, so we can address all of the fundamentally significant issues simultaneously.

— 4 —

Overcoming the Tragedy of the Commons

With the risk of nuclear war receding, the threat of our ending with a bang no longer has a chance of galvanizing us to halt our course. Our risk now is of winding down, slowly, in a whimper. Corrective action is blocked by vested interests, by well-intentioned political and business leaders, and by their electorates, all of whom are perfectly correct in not noticing big changes from year to year. Instead, each year there are just somewhat more people, and somewhat fewer resources on earth.

Jerod Diamond

*I*n this chapter we examine what is probably the most important issue society now faces—the tragedy of the commons. Our Box structure encourages us to ignore it and to limit our attention to the confines of the Game. But the tragedy cannot be ignored forever. In the end, with a Game mentality, we will destroy our soils, air quality, water tables, and the ozone layer, and thoughtlessly kill off other species, both plant and animal.

The Box system is the problem, encouraging people to see themselves as independent players, entitled to these common pool resources. It directs us to think "growth is good" and "more is better" rather than "let's figure out what we really want," or "what's really needed here?"

When common pool resources are plentiful, before the carrying capacity has been reached, our rule-of-law, constitutional, capitalist system generates productivity for most everyone. Through it, we enjoy individual freedoms and can all benefit from economic growth. But once the carrying capacity of the commons is reached, everything changes. When the grass of the commons is eaten faster than it is replenished, all us villagers are brought together into one system. We face a shared crisis that insists we become a community rather than remaining competitors. It requires that we change from a Box to a Circle system.

Within the Box system, each villager faces a simple choice: either add sheep or withhold. If he chooses to add, he receives all the benefit and bears only a small portion of the costs. The rest of those costs are "externalized" to the commons so that everyone bears them. Forced to act as an individual, this is the best option for him. His neighbors will add sheep either way, so for him to exercise restraint at this point does not stop the ultimate destruction of the commons. It just accelerates his level of suffering.

Even if many villagers do exercise restraint and refrain from adding sheep for the common good, the result of their well-meaning efforts may be to make things worse. The rest of the villagers will be oblivious, continuing with their competition and benefiting from what they see as poor business decisions on the part of their competitors. In fact, those who exercise restraint delay the necessary awakening of the system to the problem.

Today's Commons

The tragedy of the commons is a natural phenomenon affecting all life—plants, animals, and human history. The people of Easter Island faced it, as we've seen. And so did the Babylonians, Egyptians, Greeks, Romans, Mayans, and other civilizations. They all show classic signs of the problem, becoming more populated than their lands can support, less fertile and more desert-like. Key is whether they recognize what's going on and transform to some higher level of cooperation. Of course, today the limits we face are planetary. There are no other lands to look to for more resources. And there are many "tragedies" developing. Every time we fly in an airplane, do a wash, throw something "away" in the garbage, take an antibiotic, or use a weed killer, we diminish some endangered commons.

For example, we all appreciate low-cost gasoline. It allows us to enjoy inexpensive travel and cheap goods shipped from afar. But each time we benefit from this, we take from some common-pool resource. We put more pollutants into the atmosphere, encourage more land to get paved, generate more risk of global warming, negatively impact the local spirit of community, and draw down the world's oil supply.

Competing fast-food chains like McDonald's, Wendy's, and Burger King damage many commons. Tropical rain forests are cleared to make room for raising beef or for producing the millions of tons of packaging that goes with this food. This packaging then becomes garbage for the landfill commons or adds to the litter along roadside commons. In pursuit of the uniform French fry, the diversity of potato species, another common asset, is diminished, and pesticides are used which seep into the water supply. While all these priceless commons are being damaged, our system directs our attention not toward noticing this or protecting them, but toward cute commercials that tell us how fun and healthy all this is. Additionally, big campaign donations go to the representatives most willing to ignore the problem.

Perhaps the most important endangered commons is our general awareness and understanding. Our children are taught to associate these meals with happy clowns and playground fun. In the process, we lose our respect for animals, our government, the environment, and even ourselves.

In England, when five people passed out leaflets that explained some of the problems that fast food products can cause, McDonald's sued them for libel. Faced with the prospect of years-long court battles against well-financed corporate attorneys, most of the "offenders" immediately apologized and promised never to raise the issues again. Two, however, chose to put their lives on hold and defend themselves. McDonald's then spent over $40 million dollars on what eventually became the longest running trial in English history—before McDonalds lost the case.

Within the Game there are basically three possible responses to the tragedy of the commons: (1) implement regulations to limit the activities of the villagers; (2) change the incentives for using the commons; and (3) privatize the commons. All are within the Box and promote the Game. None works in the long run.

Box Solution #1: Regulations

Laws can be used to protect common resources. Regulations can limit pollution and zoning can limit the type of building in an area. With this strategy, all the villagers act together through government, establishing limits to their freedoms, and enforcing those limits: what Garret Hardin calls "mutual coercion."

This seems like a straightforward approach, but it doesn't always work. To protect our dwindling fish resources, for instance, one law limits commercial fishermen to working only a couple of days a year. But in response, the fishermen work dangerously hard during those two days. Other laws limit the length of fishing boats or the type of equipment that can be used. Fishermen simply build wider, less efficient boats, and invent new equipment, directing their creativity to overcoming the rules.

In his book, *The Death of Common Sense: How Laws are Suffocating America*, Philip Howard says, "Our regulatory system has become an instruction manual. It tells us and the bureaucrats exactly what to do and how to do it. Detailed rule after detailed rule addresses every eventuality, or at least every situation lawmakers and bureaucrats can think of." He adds, "Modern law has not protected us from stupidity and caprice but has made stupidity and caprice dominant features of our society."

An old adage says, "You can't legislate morality." But since legislation is practically the only tool we have in the Box system, we often try anyway.

Unfortunately, the way we determine these laws is not well suited to protecting the commons. The special interest battle is just another set of villagers on a different commons, all dipping from the public good. I once experienced an example of how this works in a small neighborhood. The city council was attempting to manage the street-commons in the city by distributing automobile traffic more fairly. The council proposed opening a connecting street through one of the more affluent neighborhoods. But naturally, the people who lived there were upset with the proposal and fought the idea. On one hand, they were just parents trying to ensure the safety of their children, but they were also a special interest group doing battle against the general interest.

During the final decision-making meeting, the city council faced a room full of angry people from the affected neighborhood. No one from the general public was there since the change affected them only slightly. So one speaker after another rose to protest the proposal. Mothers spoke in tears about the added risk to their children. Everyone remarked how unfair it was that tax money should be used to impose something on people when they didn't want it. The goodhearted but beleaguered city council was overmatched and the idea was abandoned.

The competitive process for making collective decisions will not protect the commons. Special interests will win over the general interest because, by design, the general interest has no voice.

If a general interest group ever does get formed and organized, like environmentalists, for instance, the system redefines and marginalizes them. It turns them into, not the voice of the people, but just another competitor. And because this group has less money to reach the media than other special interests, their voice gets little notice unless they resort to attention-grabbing gimmicks like demonstrations. Then they are characterized as oddballs and radicals, while the well-dressed, well-paid lawyers and public relations consultants of the special interests seem thoughtful and responsible.

In the end, even if good laws are made to protect common resources, they restrict freedoms, add inefficiencies to our work, orient us away from the pressing need to protect the resource, and make us frustrated with government. At best, they are only a stop-gap measure or a complement to other strategies.

Box Solution #2: Incentives

Another strategy for heading off a tragedy of the commons is for government to structure new incentives. Charging fees, imposing taxes, or providing rewards can promote desired behaviors. For example, national parks now charge a fee for admission. This is partly to raise revenue, but it is also designed to reduce the demand for these overburdened parks and preserve them.

Taxes are imposed on polluters to change the scoring of the Game and influence corporate decisions. Medical insurers use incentives that are more complex. A typical insurance plan requires the policyholder to pay for covered medical expenses until a deductible is reached. After that, the policy pays 80 percent until some higher number is reached. Then the plan pays for all eligible costs. This approach seeks to protect the common pool of health dollars that subscribers have paid.

Even if carefully designed and implemented incentives work to affect behaviors perfectly, they undermine desired attitudes. They encourage "gaming the system," where people follow the letter of the law rather than the spirit of the law. They encourage doing what is expedient, not what is right, and undermine everyone's natural relationship to the common good. So, for example, once people meet their insurance deductibles, they tend to overuse the health resource pool. Such incentives encourage people to be extrinsically, rather than intrinsically-motivated. People feel less concern about what is morally right or what they really want, and more driven by the incentives of the Game.

Box Solution #3: Private Property

The solution used in England for the "bare as a commons" problem was the Enclosure Acts, where the Crown gave the land that had been commons to the aristocracy. Then, anyone caught hunting or grazing sheep on these newly-private lands could be punished for trespassing and theft.

Although this solution caused great hardship for many, at least it protected the grounds. Private landowners will naturally preserve the long-term health of their own land. They will make the necessary investments to help the lands recover. This privatization of what should be public ends the competition over those lands. It maintains the overall Game, although of course, it is now patently unfair.

One of the modern ways to privatize a commons is through quotas, to allocate portions of the commons to particular users. With such a quota, you are allowed to emit a certain amount of pollution or to catch a certain number of fish in this year's season. The key is to make as much money as possible from your allocation.

This approach protects the commons for a time, but it also promotes gaming the system. In a Northwest example, aluminum companies were given quotas of low cost electric power from hydroelectric dams, largely to provide high paying jobs in rural areas. But in May 2000, energy prices soared and utility companies were scrambling to find power. So the aluminum companies shut down their plants and resold power (given to them at prices below cost) back to the same utility companies, in some cases for twenty-two times what it cost to produce.

The Circle Solution: Choice-creating

A few years ago, I was talking to a fisherman in Scotland. When I asked him about the fishing quotas in his area, he said, "Oh, you have to go around the rules here, or you can't make a living." Then he added, "The people who fish need to make the rules. We fishermen used to decide on what we should catch and everyone went along. But now the government does it, and we all feel they are trying to screw us."

To avert the tragedy of the commons the villagers, or the fishermen in this case, should decide the rules of the game. But more importantly, they should talk regularly, building goodwill and a sense of shared purpose. To genuinely solve the tragedy of the commons, we must escape from the Box system.

Of course, one way to shift from the Box system is to fall backwards into the Triangle structure, where some person, organization, or government owns all the resources. This is the likely place we will end up if we wait too long to address this issue. An environmentalist I once talked with was fearful about this result. He said, "I don't see how democracy can survive the tragedy of the commons."

Or maybe there is a way to shift to the methods of pre-history, where diverse peoples naturally cooperated to protect the shared water hole, the limited fruit-bearing trees, or scarce game. When people can see and recognize the threat to common-pool resources, even enemies can begin to cooperate and create new cultural norms. Today there are a number of anarchists, Libertarians, and community activists who believe that we can abolish protective legislation and bureaucracy, and trust in the natural propensity of people to work together.

But things are more complex today. The Box system keeps us from our natural propensity to cooperate with our neighbors, aiming us to compete instead. We must go forward to the Circle system. We need to structure a whole-system, Choice-creating conversation.

A number of years ago, I experienced an example of how Choice-creating, can resolve the tragedy of the commons. I went to the storage closet to get two easels I needed for a meeting. They were gone. Technically, they belonged to our department, but over time, they had become common property. Anxiously, I searched and found them. Someone from another department was using them to hold signs for a large gathering of people. Time was short as I told her I needed them. She balked.

There was an awkward moment as we both focused on our separate needs for this limited common resource. Then I had the good sense to say out loud what I was thinking, "Let's see. Do I really need both of these?" Almost immediately, I realized that the meeting room we were using was very small and I'd be better off just hanging large sheets of paper on the walls and not taking up space with the easels. I started to tell her when she suddenly responded, describing something that would work better for her as well. In that brief interchange, we had shifted from competing over a scarce resource to Choice-creating. Then we went from being short two easels, to having two too many. By thinking this way, it was as if we had miraculously materialized four easels, and even better, we grew in our relationship.

To convene a series of Choice-creating meetings for the whole system is a strategy for overcoming the tragedy of the commons. Not only will breakthroughs happen, but the process itself will forge a community spirit and a right relationship with the commons. Regulations, incentives, or quotas may emerge from these meetings, but the larger purpose is to promote an orientation to the *spirit* of the law as being more important than the letter of the law.

This solution does not necessarily mean dropping laws or law-making procedures already in place. Nor does it mean that people are being asked to sacrifice or to cooperate. It only means that they engage with others regularly to see if there aren't new and better solutions than what we already know. New options, new attitudes, new feelings, new perspectives will emerge.

For us to recognize that the Citizens Amendment will solve the all-important tragedy of the commons, there are still some questions to answer: 1) How can Choice-creating make such a substantial difference? 2) How can we involve everyone in the nation in a conversation that is Choice-creating? 3) How will it work with transnational corporations as the villagers on the commons? and 4) How can an amendment to the U.S. Constitution affect planetary commons? These questions will be answered in subsequent chapters.

Part II

NECESSARY UNDERSTANDINGS

Willingly to turn over to a mechanical system the question of how our living culture will develop is a form of idolatry. Not impersonal forces, but their only real alternative—collective human decisions—should govern our destiny.

Andrew Bard Schmookler, *The Illusion of Choice: How the Market Economy Shapes Our Destiny*

— 5 —

Choice-creating and Dynamic Facilitation

There is a "movement in the air"—an exciting renaissance of interest in conversation as a transformational tool, and its potential as a wellspring for much-needed social change.

Rosa Zubizarreta

ocial philosopher Tom Atlee recently began a talk by asking the audience five questions:

1. How many of you have been in a really productive conversation where the people involved were seeing the topic in new ways and seeing options and possibilities that none of you had thought of before? (About half raised their hands.)
2. How many of you know of groups or organizations where you find LOTS of that kind of conversation? (About a fifth raised their hands.)

3. How many of you know of an elected democratic government whose decisions you feel are truly wise? (A few—Denmark and Iceland were mentioned.)
4. How many of you think we will survive the 21st Century if we don't put a lot of wisdom into our collective decision-making and problem-solving? (None.)
5. How many of you believe it is possible for ordinary people to generate wisdom together? (Everyone.)

Tom's questions laid out the issue beautifully. We know it's possible to have Choice-creating conversations, where creativity and wisdom happen among ordinary people and where decisions get made jointly. We long for it in small groups, in large organizations, and in nations. But it doesn't happen very often.

Recently, a young woman was telling me how frustrated she was with Congress—how childish and argumentative elected representatives seem, and how they don't address the truly important issues. Then she ended by apologizing. I asked her why she apologized and she said, "I don't like to talk about politics because I don't like that way of talking."

She's right. Our official collective way of talking, thinking, and deciding issues is not pretty. It's a battle rather than a collaboration. As Deborah Tannen says in her book, *The Argument Culture: Stopping America's War of Words*, we have a "pervasive warlike atmosphere that makes us approach public dialogue, and just about anything we need to accomplish, as if it were a fight." But this combative style arises, not because people are selfish or that our culture is argumentative, as many people think, but because we have structured it that way. Majority rule, for instance, pretty much guarantees a back and forth argument between two positions, rather than thoughtful reflection.

When we don't structure for Choice-creating, it is difficult to achieve. It's not just a matter of everyone trying harder. So instead of seeking this creative, wisdom-generating conversation, people often strive for second best, to be dispassionate, logical and under control. But this means blocking our true feelings, undermining our relationships with others, and risking that our emotions work against rather than with us.

But, as the answers to Tom's questions suggest, we need for ordinary people to generate wisdom together, something most of us believe is possible. How do we do it? And how does the Citizens Amendment help us?

Two Kinds of Talking

To understand how to generate wisdom, we need to recognize the difference between two ways of talking: transactional (TA) and transformational (TF). TA talking is a transmission of information between sender and receiver. It is as though bits of information are exchanged and added to a database each person carries inside. TF talking, on the other hand, is a heart-to-heart experience where people and concepts evolve together. Participants in a TF conversation might be "moved" by the experience or find it "deeply meaningful."

A friend of mine told me a story that illustrates the difference. She was in a movie theater and noticed a young girl and her mother sitting directly behind her. After awhile, she felt something touch her hair and, eventually, she discovered that the young girl had deliberately stuck gum in it. When the movie was over, my friend confronted the child and parent. The girl's mother was horrified to learn what had happened, turned to her daughter, and demanded she apologize. A dutiful "I'm sorry" was all she got. This apology meant little under the pressure of her mother's insistence. It was a transactional communication.

Outside the movie ten minutes later, as my friend was about to get into her car, she heard a child's voice call to her. Apparently, the girl had time to think about what she had done, and on her own ran over and said, "I'm really sorry." They were almost the same words, but this time they came from the heart. My friend's frustration melted. Both people were moved. It was a transformational communication.

Each mode has value and engenders a different sort of thinking. With TA talking, we spark critical thinking, judging, analyzing, sorting, combining, storing, and relaying information. With it we can influence others toward predetermined goals. In a TF conversation, outcomes are reached spontaneously, through breakthroughs, insights, or changes of heart. The whole person is involved—creativity, reason, emotions, body, and spirit.

The word "apology" only has meaning in a TF conversation. This is also true of "consensus," "community," and "democracy," because these words require the genuine involvement of people. The word "involve" comes from the root "to turn inside of." To be involved means engaging fully with others in a process that creates trust, relationship, meaningfulness, and shared commitment. It is more than just providing input, being listened to, or voting. It requires a transformational, authentic conversation.

Nobel Prize-winning quantum physicist David Bohm uses the words "discussion" and "dialogue" to point to a similar distinction. He explains that "discussion" has the same root as "percussion" and "concussion." The root "cuss" means "to strike" or to "break things up." In his book, *On Dialogue*, Bohm says, "Discussion is almost like a ping pong game, where people are batting the ideas back and forth and the object of the game is to win points for yourself."

The word, "dialogue," on the other hand, derives from the roots "dia" which means "through," and "logos" which means "the word" or "the meaning of the word." Thus, in dialogue, shared meaning emerges through words. Dialogue elicits shared understandings, personal growth, and group coherence.

Bohm taught a particular practice of dialogue, with twenty to forty people assembling on a regular basis, with no purpose or agenda. They suspend judgment and inquire into a topic, watching the

Two Kinds of Talking

Transactional (TA)

- Focus: *What* is said ... the content.
- Transmitting information—where concepts and information are exchanged, modified or evaluated.
- People remain the same, although they improve their skills or have new understandings.
- People remain detached from the "things" they talk about and the people they talk with.
- The process can be predetermined, step by step, as with an agenda.
- The results (knowledge, skills, decisions, etc.) are measurable.
- Associated words: Discussion, input, training, team, compromise, agreement, and decision-making.

Transformational (TF)

- Focus: *How* it is said ... the process.
- Creating new information—where concepts, information, and people all evolve together.
- People are "moved" by the experience, and become different in a meaningful way.
- People are fully involved—builds trust and a sense of "we".
- The process is necessarily *dynamic* (e.g., you go with the flow).
- Measurable results are often far greater than TA results, but measuring them can diminish them.
- Associated words: Dialogue, involvement, education, community, consensus, and Choice-creating.

Chart #5

group's process and challenging assumptions. It can sometimes be a frustrating two hours, because it often doesn't seem like the group is getting anywhere, but at the same time, an exciting new form of group coherence and collective intelligence also can emerge.

Another form of dialogue is the more heartfelt approach of the *Guild for Psychological Studies* in San Francisco, which has been conducting seminars since the 1940's. In this form, a facilitator takes more of a leadership role, asking evocative questions and encouraging participants to speak only what they are discovering in the moment, not what they already know. There are other forms of transformational talking as well, including psychotherapy, prayer, personal sharing, and Choice-creating.

The two different modes of talking and thinking, transactional and transformational, are analogous to ways in which physicists view nature. The traditional physicist sees the universe in a transactional way as a machine which can be measured and analyzed by objective observers. But quantum physicists and cosmologists see the universe more as a living process with fields of energy and the potential for spontaneous change. "Discussion" fits with Newton's mechanical universe, and "dialogue" belongs to the quantum view. Bohm suggests that when people engage in dialogue and, presumably, other forms of transformational talking, they are actually changing the "nature of thought itself." He says about dialogue, "When you listen to somebody else, whether you like it or not, what they say becomes part of you."

The distinction between transactional and transformational talking may not seem apparent or important to us today, but it was always important to ancient peoples. Native Americans, for example, used the peace pipe, the kiva, the talking stick, the vision quest, and sacred dances to call forth the spirit of transformational talking. They structured their lives so that important decisions, particularly for the tribe, would always be made in this spirit.

Today, we do the opposite and structure TA thinking and talking for those big decisions. In politics, in our education system, in corporations, and in most organizations, we focus more on measurable results and deny the existence of this deeper way of talking. We take TF concepts like "involvement" and "democracy" and redefine them so that they fit into the transactional mold. For instance, we say that citizens are "involved" because they can vote and, therefore, the country is a "democracy." This simplistic perspective limits the magical possibilities.

Choice-creating vs. Decision-making

Wise decisions and true democracy arise from TF talking but not necessarily from dialogue. Bohm and the practitioners of his form of dialogue suggest that a group should use dialogue to build a foundation for decision-making, but switch to discussion for making decisions. The word to "de-cide" means "to cut away" the bad alternatives, leaving the good. Choice-creating is different, offering us a way to reach joint conclusions through TF talking. Chart #6 describes the two different styles.

To illustrate how Choice-creating can be structured instead of decision-making, let me describe an old role-playing exercise used in business training sessions. (See *Supervisory and Executive Development,* by N. R. F. Maier, A. Solem, and A. A. Maier, ©1957 by John Wiley and Sons.) Four volunteers are chosen. Three play the role of employees in a manufacturing company, with three different jobs, while one plays the boss. The workers are happy in their work, taking turns on the three jobs. But in private, the boss is given some new information: A 50% gain in productivity would be achieved if, rather than rotating between jobs, each employee stayed on the job he does best. The exercise begins when the boss calls a meeting to discuss this new possibility.

Two Kinds of Thinking

Decision-making

- It's a critical thinking process … e.g., choosing the best from a set of different options.

- This process can be codified into a procedure, agenda, or set of criteria. The process can be managed so that people stay "on task."

- Decision-making meetings are rarely satisfying. The real issue often goes unaddressed. People don't feel heard, their passion is squelched, creativity is muted, and vital energy is squandered on agree/disagree discussions. It takes a long time to reach agreement.

- Decisions get reached through logic, compromise, power plays, or a voting. True consensus, win/win decisions, or high levels of commitment are rare.

- There is emotional safety because you don't let go of your role.

Choice-creating

- It's a creative thinking process … e.g., seeking a breakthrough option that is better than available options.

- This process must be dynamic. You have to "just know it" when it happens. It must be facilitated, not managed.

- Choice-creating meetings are satisfying once people get used to this approach. The real issue is addressed. People are authentic, open-minded, open-hearted, learning, engaged, efficient, creative, and respectful. And it takes less time to reach joint conclusions.

- Decisions get reached via shifts of mind and heart. Breakthrough results are expected. Byproducts are: trust, understanding, consciousness, empowerment, community, etc.

- It feels risky because you are emotionally vulnerable.

Chart #6

The role-playing goes one of two ways. If the boss *proposes the new approach* and asks the employees what they think, they will have a transactional conversation. They will do "decision-making," discussing back and forth whether to try it or not. In the end, they will decide yes or no—or some half-measure, like trying it for a while to see.

If, however, the boss *presents the new information* and asks the employees what they think, the resulting conversation will usually be Choice-creating. The four will seek to understand the issue, listen to one another's feelings and needs, and will become creative in addressing them. Most always, they will discover or invent some new alternative that suits everyone. Some of these solutions are: two people switching jobs while one remains; each of the three alternating among his two best jobs; all switching jobs for unequal periods of time; or the boss helping out.

So with decision-making, people tend to go back and forth agreeing and disagreeing, trying to influence one another. When a decision is ultimately reached, it is to a preformed option for which there may be little enthusiasm or commitment. But with Choice-creating, there is an engaging conversation. Trust builds, relationships strengthen, people grow, breakthrough solutions emerge, and a consensus evolves for which there is natural commitment. It almost makes you wonder why we'd ever do anything else.

Overcoming a Crisis

To engage in Choice-creating is like encountering a crisis. You face a problem that you really care about and to which there is no satisfactory answer. It is not a negotiation between two positions or a selection among alternatives. It's messier than that. It requires that you open yourself, be creative, and trust that, in the end, something will happen that allows for committed consensus. This kind of openness can be threatening if there is any risk of judgment present.

In the same way that judgment stifles the creativity of people who are brainstorming ideas off the tops of their heads, it also stifles the heartfelt creativity of Choice-creating. People cannot be open and authentic, or grow and change in their views if judgment is present.

In Choice-creating, crises are overcome through different kinds of breakthroughs, new inventions, new understandings of the problem, new feelings and attitudes, or through an elevation of consciousness. The great Swiss psychiatrist, Carl Jung, talked about these breakthroughs in consciousness: "All the greatest and most important problems of life are fundamentally insoluble. They must be so, for they express the necessary polarity inherent in every self-regulating system. They can never be solved, but only outgrown. . . . This outgrowing proved on further investigation to be a new level of consciousness. Some higher or wider interest appeared on the patient's horizon, and through this broadening of his outlook the insoluble problem lost its urgency. It was not solved logically in its own terms, but faded out when confronted with a new and stronger life urge. It was not repressed and made unconscious, but merely appeared in a different light, and so really did become different. What, on a lower level, had led to the wildest conflicts and to panicky outbursts of emotion, from the higher level of personality now looked like a storm in the valley seen from the mountain top. This does not mean that the storm is robbed of its reality, but instead of being in it one is above it."

Most meetings are aimed at decision-making rather than Choice-creating. We prepare agendas, define goals, and use step-by-step techniques to keep people on track—all of which seem like common sense. However, by structuring this form of talking, we unknowingly narrow our thinking, diminish ourselves, and limit the possibilities for change.

Consider what happened at a meeting I recently observed. A group was organizing itself and the moderator suggested that there were two alternatives for how people could decide issues: voting or consensus. Then he defined "consensus" as when everyone votes "yes" with no more than two people abstaining. Unknowingly, just by presenting these two well-defined alternatives he was assuring a transactional rather than a transformational conversation. And worse, if the group adopted either of these two proposals, it was structuring future conversations to be transactional as well.

The group went back and forth over the two options. Everyone wanted consensus, but knew something wasn't right with these options. In the end, they didn't decide. They changed topics. If the moderator had been on the ball, he might have realized that this was the group's decision and that it was an example of true consensus. A skilled facilitator might've jumped in and said, "It seems that you all want to decide issues in a less formal way than has been proposed, through talking things over and just seeing where people stand. Is that right?" In response, the group probably would have replied, "Yes!" in one unanimous voice.

Choice-creating encourages this in-the-moment, "sense of the meeting" type of conclusion which captures what everyone wants, but which may not fit into predetermined box-like expectations. With Choice-creating, the aim is not for people to stay on topic within some set of boundaries, but to follow group energy to a point where everyone looks at one another, knowing they want the same thing. When this occurs, it's unbelievably powerful.

Choice-creating is when people *address an issue they care about deeply* in a way that allows them to be:

- *Authentic* — There are no roles or hidden agendas.
- *Open-minded* — People are interested in new and different ideas.
- *Open-hearted* — People are listening deeply to the feelings and perspectives of each person and they are being influenced in response.

- *Learning* — Each person is interested and seeks out new understandings.
- *Engaged* — Everyone is involved, wants to participate, and offers his or her talents.
- *Respectful* — Each person's ideas and uniqueness are appreciated.
- *Creative* — Breakthrough insights and changes of heart are frequent.
- *Efficient* — Consensus decisions are arrived at with relative speed and ease through naturally-occurring breakthroughs.

Unfortunately, many people have not experienced this kind of meeting. In the "My Turn" Column of *Newsweek* magazine (Sept. 9, 1985), Isadore Barmash described the extent of the problem by concluding: "After a lifetime of work, I've never seen a meeting end happily." One counterexample is that, for over three hundred years, the Quakers have been holding business meetings aimed at transformational talking, at true consensus. Called "meetings for worship for business," they rely on participants sharing two religious assumptions: 1) Every person has "that of God" within, and 2) He or she is "seeking God's Truth." For the process to work, everyone must adhere to these assumptions. Consensus is sought, not so much as a polling of the collected wisdom of those present, but as a collective discernment of God's will. (See "An introduction to Quaker Business Meetings" by Eden Grace.) Besides requiring that all participants share one religious perspective, Quakers also use a "clerk of the meeting" to act as a kind of facilitator. She asks for moments of silence, reflects on group progress, and proposes postponements on difficult topics.

The Dynamic Facilitator Assures Choice-creating

One way to generate group Choice-creating that works better than relying on a shared belief system is with the help of a "Dynamic Facilitator." Unfortunately, the word "facilitator" is another TF term that has been given TA meaning. Most people have come to expect that a facilitator keeps them to an agenda, holds them on task, or helps them to follow a step-by-step procedure. I distinguish this kind of facilitation, which is aimed at helping people do decision-making, from Dynamic Facilitation, which supports people to do Choice-creating. The Dynamic Facilitator helps people make progress in jumps, creative insights, and spontaneous changes of heart.

I've developed a specific approach to Dynamic Facilitation that will need its own book. But for our purposes here, twelve principles are described below.

1) Distinguish between process and content. The group determines the content—*what* is talked about. They generate the results. The facilitator focuses on the process—*how* people talk. She assures Choice-creating rather than decision-making.

2) Help people attend to the issue, not other people. The Dynamic Facilitator uses a flip chart or large screen to direct the attention of participants toward the front of the room. In this way, everyone works on the issue, not each other.

3) Help the group assume ownership of the issue. People in the group should be working on what they care about, regardless of whether or not it seems impossible to solve. In transactional conversations, the tendency is to pick something that is solvable or some issue that has been assigned. But here, the Dynamic Facilitator helps people choose what they most care about.

85

4) Use reflection. The Dynamic Facilitator reflects back to people what they are saying or seem to be feeling. She does this by using flip charts to paraphrase or capture the points made. This active listening process eliminates miscommunication and, more importantly, stimulates breakthroughs. Through reflection, for example, people discover what they really want and grow from this discovery.

5) Orient the conversation to numbered lists of Solutions, Problem-statements, Data, Concerns, and Decisions. Lists help people to think generatively and let go of points once they are made. For instance, the Dynamic Facilitator might begin by asking, "What are some of the issues we *might* address?" as opposed to, "Does anyone have an issue?" This suggests that there are an infinite number of issues rather than one or two.

In particular, four lists are crucial: Solutions, Concerns, Data, and Problem-statements. With these, the facilitator can turn every comment into a contribution. If someone starts to criticize an idea, the Dynamic Facilitator would rephrase the criticism as a concern and get it down on that list. Then she might say to that person, "It sounds as if, behind your concern, you have a different idea for how to solve this." Usually there is another idea that can be added to the list of possible solutions. Once a consensus begins to emerge, it can be added to the list of Decisions (or Conclusions, or Next Steps).

6) Purge initial answers. When confronted with a big issue, most people already have some kind of opinion. These opinions must be fully expressed and captured, usually on the list of Solutions, in a way that people know they have been heard. If not, creativity will be blocked. In traditional meetings, it is easy to become polarized into agree/disagree camps when people express their ideas. Here, the Dynamic

Facilitator heads this off by helping each person express their views fully, and then to seek more options.

7) Protect people from all forms of judgment. When people are being creative, judgment in any form is harmful. For example, if someone is expressing his view and is cut off by a comment about why his idea won't work, the facilitator must act quickly to keep him safe. She captures the original idea as one possible solution and also captures the criticism as a concern. She makes sure both people are fully heard and both views are respected.

8) Go with the energy of the group. In a transformational conversation, new solution ideas can come to the minds of participants at any moment. The Dynamic Facilitator must "go with the flow" and encourage this spontaneity. She can use the lists to help build energy. By capturing all comments, she helps people see that whatever comes to mind and whatever anyone says is an asset to the group.

In a Choice-creating conversation, there is often a pattern to how energy unfolds. Once people purge their initial solutions, they tend to become more circumspect. They start noticing other aspects of the problem and do more problem-solving. The facilitator should be sensitive to this change in group energy and, on occasion, help this shift to happen. Then, someone is liable to say, "I'm not sure we are solving the real problem."

This questioning attitude can spark breakthroughs. Everyone stops for a moment, often realizing that interests and perspectives have changed, and that the group's issue may now be different.

9) Diverge/converge. In Choice-creating, the facilitator helps people generate many ideas and then helps them narrow the list down to one, or just a few. Diverging and converging may happen a number of times before the group consensus becomes apparent. The best way to converge is not through deciding on one option, but via a breakthrough that everyone supports.

10) Orient the group toward creating versus deciding. In Choice-creating, it is important that people make minimal use of judging. When narrowing down the list, for instance, instead of having the group decide from among three possibilities, it is better if the facilitator can help them create a fourth idea, which combines all three, or which works even better.

11) Suggest different activities and venues. To be creative, people must think in different ways, using different parts of the mind. At times, the Dynamic Facilitator may suggest that everyone pause to stretch, or to write down responses to a question, or to talk together in small groups. These different venues can help maintain group energy and spark new insights. Even when people break into small groups, the spirit of Choice-creating remains; for example, the decision-making words "agree" and "disagree" are not heard.

12) Highlight and celebrate progress. It is more difficult for people to assess progress in a transformational meeting than in one that is transactional, since breakthroughs cannot be foreseen or their importance readily measured. People change in TF sessions, so when a group resolves what was once thought to be an impossible-to-solve problem, they tend to discount their amazing progress. Looking back, everything seems so obvious they often berate themselves for not seeing it sooner. The facilitator should act as a kind of historian, recounting how the group's thinking unfolded, reminding everyone how exceptional they have been, and helping them to celebrate progress.

At the end of each meeting, the group's progress should be captured in clear statements. These statements serve as symbols of the group's work that can carry momentum forward.

How Dynamic Facilitation Works

The Dynamic Facilitator begins a Wisdom Council by asking, "What are some of the issues you *might* like to talk about?" She helps the group develop a list and narrow it to what they want to work on first.

The selected issue need not be well-defined and, in fact, can be just be a statement of feelings or even a couple of issues combined. Rather than trying to define the problem further, the Dynamic Facilitator helps people express whatever it is they have to say about it. Often they express a frustration, like "we can't do anything about this," or a particular solution approach like, "government should just get off people's backs," or "the key is education," or "people just need to respect one another."

Instead of trying to direct people to defining the problem, as logic would dictate, the Dynamic Facilitator helps them to express whatever point they are making. Usually this point can be added to the list of Solutions. She will invite them to flesh out their thoughts by asking, "How would you suggest we do that?" followed by, "What would be the next step after that?" until the person has expressed the point fully. We call this "the purge."

Once the points are fully expressed and people feel they've been heard, they are more able to open their minds, listen to the points of others, and try out new perspectives. When the issue is a difficult one, the frequent result of the group's purge is for everyone to see that all known answers are inadequate. Energy is less lively at this point, maybe with periods of silence and anxiety that nothing can be done. Then someone will mention a curious bit of new information, or ask a question. The energy will shift to become more like solving a puzzle than reeling from a crisis.

One form of breakthrough that often happens at this stage is when the group realizes that there is a more fundamental question or problem than the one with which they started. Someone will say, "the real problem is . . . " and energy will build. Someone will wonder "what do we really want here?" or "what would happen if . . . " and the group is on its way to a breakthrough.

One group from my seminars was concerned about the loss of traditional family values. Several people started expressing their frustration with parents who rely on schools or television to raise their kids. Others complained about the media teaching violence and sex. One person stated strongly that one of the parents should stay home with the kids. Another said that we need to make sure there are enough high paying jobs so that one parent can stay home. Another thought that religious institutions held the key. Still others felt that it was important to educate parents in how to raise their children. Each view was fully heard, but the Dynamic Facilitator made sure no one view became the focus. Instead, as each person's perspective was expressed, the group arrived at a difficult, empty stage where the problem seemed overwhelming.

Then someone began to talk from the heart about their own family, their own upbringing, and how difficult it was for them to raise children with the same quality of support they had received from their parents. Others in the group responded by sharing on a deep level as well, and began to talk about their struggles with time, increased financial pressures, and the lack of a supportive community. These heartfelt remarks changed the tone in the room. As people shared their experiences, group members became curious about the differences between yesterday and today. They considered the impact of cell phones, the media, and the Internet. The conversation became lively again. At one point, everyone arrived at the realization that today's challenges are quite different from those in the past. It was a breakthrough for them that maybe what was needed was a different kind of family. At the end of the hour, they had redefined the problem. Their collective energy had shifted to this larger, more ambitious issue: "How can we create a society where everyone feels included, as though belonging to one family?" Interestingly, to them this bigger issue didn't seem as overwhelming as saving the traditional family, and they felt excited to continue working on it.

With a traditional facilitator aimed at decision-making, it is unlikely that either issue—the loss of family values or the creation of a global family—would have been addressed in the first place. Equipped with only logical thinking and control-oriented approaches, traditional decision-making gives us a limited range of problem-solving capability. It avoids emotional issues, impossible-to-solve issues, and problems that are outside our area of expertise or responsibility. But with Dynamic Facilitation and the prospect of Choice-creating, people can address what is really important to them, regardless of how hard it seems—and expect breakthroughs.

Because people grow in perspective and capability when they do Choice-creating, the process itself often becomes the solution. For example, many times I've facilitated groups working on the issue of "low trust in the organization." Over the course of just three or four meetings, after people have expressed their frustrations and worked together to find new solutions, they usually look around the room and realize they don't have that issue anymore. They all trust each other and often can hardly remember why the problem originally came up.

The Constitution Establishes Decision-making

Despite the huge benefits to be gained from Choice-creating, its use is relatively rare. This is largely because decision-making is imposed on us by the system in which we live. Consider the constitutional system with its balance of power, rule of law, elected representatives, voting, majority rule, adversarial legal structure, and Parliamentary Procedure.

Elected representatives can't engage in a transformational conversation because, for the most part, they must adhere to the party line or to a set of predefined positions. They can't be open-minded or open-hearted on these issues or they will lose the support of key constituents. So they take pride in *not* changing their minds, in being consistent, and they become masters of Parliamentary game playing.

Voting sets up decision-making very much like the foreman did in the exercise when he presented his proposal, rather than sharing the data. In voting, specific ideas are presented, people debate them back and forth, and then they make their decision. Those in the minority are overruled, no consensus is sought, and creative thinking is discouraged.

Of course, the judicial system is entirely transactional. It is an adversarial process where decisions are made according to preset standards. The whole process is a competition. The kinds of questions it addresses are: Did this person break the law or not? Or, is this law constitutional or not? There is no concern about what would be best for everyone, for what people really want, or for reaching consensus. It's combat within the rules.

Parliamentary Procedure is transactional as well. In its time, it was a wonderful innovation, laying out publicly, for the first time, exactly how decisions were to be made. But the process is so inefficient that no corporation would make decisions this way. It's another case of trying to be rational and straightforward, but getting something far less. With it, there is no room for breakthrough insights. If one did miraculously occur, it would be ruled out of order and immediately squelched.

Furthermore, our official transactional mode of talking extends far beyond politics. It affects town council meetings, school board meetings, courtroom proceedings, Hollywood scriptwriters, and how businesses operate. It drives away TF by assuming agendas, measures, and the methods of control. Any time we are measured against set standards, like the threat of lawsuits, conversations become transactionalized. Gradually, this systemic effect has come between doctors and patients, teachers and students, and employees and management in companies.

Of course, TA talking has value. There are many times when conveying information or engaging in decision-making is appropriate. But it causes problems when it is used inappropriately, when TF is needed. When people are in conflict, when people seek meaning or the involvement of others, or when problems seem overwhelming, TA talking cannot produce the desired results. It doesn't work when we need to go straight to the heart of the matter and talk about what is really going on.

Equipped with only transactional talking, we do not face the most important issues. We ignore them and, instead, focus on the kind of smaller issues that TA talking can address. It's like the old story of the man who loses his key and looks, not where he loses it, but under the lamp because the light is better there. Author and physicist, Fritjof Capra, describes the situation: "The Earth's forests are receding, while its deserts are expanding. Topsoil on our crop lands is diminishing, and the ozone layer, which protects us from harmful ultraviolet radiation, is being depleted. Concentrations of heat-trapping gases in the atmosphere are rising, while the numbers of plant and animal species are shrinking. World population continues to grow, and the gap between the rich and the poor continues to widen. And yet, while public awareness of all these problems is rising dramatically everywhere, they are strikingly absent from the American political dialogue."

With the Citizens Amendment, the old TA structures in our system—like representatives, voting, the legal system, and Parliamentary Procedure—all remain. It's just that the Citizens Amendment adds a TF conversation and places it in a position of overall importance.

It assures the shift from decision-making to Choice-creating through simple structural devices—like the father adding the word "please," or like the foreman presenting the *problem* instead of the *solution*. The *random sampling process*, for instance, brings together ordinary people who speak only for themselves. Unlike representatives, they can grow and change in their views. When they do, it's exciting and cause for celebration. Also, because the Wisdom Council is enacted as *an amendment to the Constitution,* the people it gathers are not a special interest group. They are placed outside of politics to form We the People, a general interest group. The *required unanimity* of the Wisdom Council disallows competition or power plays, and promotes cooperation. This assures that everyone's views will be heard and respected.

These seemingly small changes may be enough to make the necessary difference. But in addition, a *capable facilitator* is provided who, even if this person is not skilled in Dynamic Facilitation, can pretty much guarantee Choice-creating instead of decision-making.

— 6 —

The Wisdom Council

and Whole-system Resonance

We predict—and there is evidence to support this—that twenty years from now a variety of processes and technologies will exist to involve large numbers of people in effective collaborative problem solving and decision making.

Michael Doyle and David Straus, *How to Make Meetings Work (1976)*

*O*n the evening of May 9, 1993, I was half-watching television and half-mulling society's problems. Suddenly, I leaped out of my chair, arms raised with excitement. In that moment, I knew that what I now call the "Citizens Amendment" would work.

Since then, I've come to realize that this same process can also be used with other large systems: cities, towns, hospitals, high schools, government agencies, professional organizations, unions, nations, and transnational corporations. A Wisdom Council in your organization, for instance, would be a way to involve everyone in setting the direction for the organization.

The Twelve Features of a Wisdom Council

To achieve the promised transformation, a Wisdom Council must have all, or most all, of the following twelve features:

1. *The Wisdom Council is chartered by the people*—Those who make up the system, whether it is a student body, city, or corporation, must officially approve using the Wisdom Council. It shouldn't come into being through an executive decision of management or by some subgroup. It requires whole-system approval—or in the case of the United States, a constitutional amendment.

2. *It is a microcosm of randomly selected people*—The people on a Wisdom Council are not self-selected, elected, or appointed by some authority. Nor is there a stratified sampling process, like being sure to have equal numbers of men and women or Democrats and Republicans. They must be randomly selected so that each person speaks only for him or her self and not for any subgroup like women, Democrats, poor people, or for a geographical region.

3. *It is empowered to select and frame the issues it addresses*—Because the Wisdom Council symbolizes all people, there is no higher authority. In the case of the Citizens Amendment, for example, this group symbolizes We the People and is not subject to Congress, the president, nor even the Constitution. As boss of the system then, symbolically speaking, the Wisdom Council chooses the issues it will consider, frames them, and works on solving them.

4. *The members are chosen in a ceremony: a lottery*—In an annual, semi-annual, or quarterly lottery, each person in the organization receives a number and has a chance to be selected. This develops a vicarious sense of relationship between individuals who are selected and those who are not.

If someone is selected with a lottery number very close to yours, for example, or lives near you or has a similar job, then you have a basis for identifying with that person.

5. *It is non-coercive*—No one is forced to serve on a Wisdom Council and the results have no official power. The Wisdom Council merely presents its conclusions and then disbands. This group has power only to the extent that everyone in the system resonates with its conclusions, or at least keeps talking about them.

6. *It operates in a fishbowl*—Once Wisdom Council members have been publicly selected, they are isolated from the influence of others. But everyone in the system knows they are meeting and, if possible, all may watch or tune into some of the deliberations. This builds trust in the process as well as vicarious involvement.

7. *It is facilitated dynamically*—The quality of the conversation within the Wisdom Council is crucial. It must be Choice-creating, not decision-making. This means that people must feel safe and respected, must speak from the heart and participate creatively. A Dynamic Facilitator can assure this quality of talking.

8. *It generates unanimous statements*—The Wisdom Council strives to reach conclusions that everyone, not just those on the Wisdom Council, can fully endorse. Unlike our current system, it is not a way for the majority to impose something on the minority. Instead, this is a process of incorporating minority perspectives into something that will work for everyone. The conclusions of the Wisdom Council are written into clear, simple sentences that are presented and prominently displayed. These statements are likely to be visions, values, and shared perspectives, points that engage and inspire people. After the Wisdom Council conclusions are presented and posted, everyone has many opportunities to

comment. If some disagree with one of them, for instance, they will be motivated to speak out and the rest of us will be interested to hear that perspective. Unlike current politics, it is a process that celebrates divergent views.

9. *The results are presented in a ceremony*—The beginning and end of each Wisdom Council are public events. First, is the lottery. Then, when the Wisdom Council concludes its work, there is an immediate presentation of the final results back to the people. Everyone in the system is part of the extended audience to whom the Wisdom Council speaks. At this final presentation, Wisdom Council members also tell the story of their group, how they evolved in their thinking, what insights they had, and how they ended. The final ceremony is an exciting moment for participants, and engaging for others.

10. *Small group dialogues are convened*—Although not specifically mentioned in the Citizens Amendment, everyone will be invited to participate in small group dialogues in town halls, churches, community centers, and individual homes. All will voice their response to the presentation and the Statements of the People, so everyone is involved.

11. *The process is ongoing*—The Wisdom Council is not a one-time event. Because it is on-going, it promotes a larger, whole-system conversation. Each Wisdom Council articulates interim conclusions from this ongoing dialogue. Wisdom Council statements also provide a history of how the views of people have evolved. They provide a way to track changes of attitude and progress on issues.

12. The *process operates in parallel with normal governance structures*—The Wisdom Council does not directly change anything in the current, existing structure. It doesn't undermine top management in a company, for instance. It merely adds a periodic short-term, small-group

meeting and presentation. Follow-up actions happen through the existing structure with the support of everyone, including management.

The term "Wisdom Council" should only be used when all or most all of the above features are present. Unfortunately, when people discover the merits of Dynamic Facilitation and Choice-creating, there is a tendency to call every such meeting a "Wisdom Council." But this term is intended only for situations where the whole system is involved, not just one small group.

Whole-system Resonance

Today we say a country is a "democracy" because the people in it mark a ballot. Usually you are presented with only two viable candidates and those of us who vote, which is often a small percentage, choose the lesser of two evils. Your views don't carry much weight. Even a near consensus of the people, as some surveys show, may not matter in the eventual decisions our political system delivers.

The Wisdom Council adds a small group meeting process to the existing system of governance. It also structures things so that the whole system resonates with this small group—where all of us in a company, city, county, or nation participate in the conversation—even though there may be thousands or millions of us. It's everyone "visiting" together on the important issues, figuring out what is best, and articulating joint conclusions.

Let's explore how the Wisdom Council includes and involves everyone in the system. Consider these five ways:

1) Actual involvement—First, everyone in the system helps to charter the Wisdom Council. In most cases this means having the opportunity to vote on whether or not to adopt this process.

Once the Wisdom Council is adopted, each year or each quarter, everyone receives a number and participates in a lottery. Then all are invited to attend a ceremony, a viewing of the results, and to meet with others in small groups.

2) Extended involvement—The Wisdom Council speaks directly to you, suggesting actions, asking questions, and posing problems that need to be resolved. It might challenge us, for instance, to see if our workplace is ecologically sustainable or if we are truly serving the best interests of our clients. It involves us in a collective effort to make improvements.

Let's say you don't like the results of a particular Wisdom Council because you have additional information on the topic. After the Statements of the People are presented, you would feel motivated to tell others what you know. You might start by telling friends, submitting your perspective to a website discussion group, or writing a letter to the newspaper. Since your point of view is different from the vast majority of people, your view will be newsworthy and gain widespread interest.

Even though you weren't selected to be on the Wisdom Council, you are now an important part of the larger conversation. And, if your views hold up as being significant to others, they will be considered by future Wisdom Councils.

3) Symbolic involvement—A symbol is an ordinary object, statement, or event that becomes an embodiment of something else more meaningful. Symbols have great force to arouse people and bind them together. Because the Wisdom Council is a symbol of all of the people in the organization or nation, when it talks, we talk.

Consider this illustration of how a symbol works its magic. I was walking quickly the other day, trying to get some exercise, when I almost stepped on a nickel. I didn't want to slow my pace, so I didn't pick it up. After all, it was only five cents. A few moments later, however, I thought of a recurring childhood dream in which I found coins near my school. Suddenly, that nickel was not only a five-cent piece, but had been transformed into meaningful symbol from my childhood. I turned around and went back for it. This type of transformation can happen to a person or group of people, too. It happened to Lady Diana of Great Britain. At one time, she was a beautiful young woman who worked with children. But after she married Prince Charles, she became a symbol to the world, part of the much larger story of princesses, fairy tales, and all of British history.

The U.S. Constitution has a magical ability to create symbols. The President of the United States, for example, is an ordinary person made special by the Constitution. Congress and the Supreme Court are similar examples. In the same way, the Constitution can anoint an ordinary group of citizens to be a symbol of We the People.

Once the Citizens Amendment is enacted, the statements of this group are Statements of the People of the United States, like the words of the Constitution itself. What they say will be important and will be talked about for years to come. When a Wisdom Council is chartered by the people of a city, or the employees of a company, they also create a symbolic embodiment of themselves.

4) "We" involvement—A strong feeling of involvement develops when separate individuals connect enough to call themselves "we." When two people fall in love, they become a couple. When spectators watch their local baseball team, even though they aren't playing, they feel part of the team. Or when people share a heartfelt experience, like overcoming a crisis, they become a community. Similarly, through the fishbowl nature of the process, the Wisdom Council builds this spirit of "we" among a large population. Through it we all face crises together and feel pride in our joint progress.

5) Holographic involvement—Choice-creating elicits a general feeling of interconnectedness—to the larger community, to those in other countries, to the health of the biosphere, and to life itself. In a Choice-creating conversation, which the Wisdom Council encourages, we speak and act from this felt sense of connection. We are still worried about our own lives, perspectives, family, and friends, but in the spirit of Choice-creating, what is best for all is most dear.

Science tells us that this holographic perspective, where each of us is a microcosm of life, is scientifically more accurate than what has passed for "common sense," that we are all separate.

The Wisdom Council is Unique

The Wisdom Council appears to be very much like other approaches that encourage greater democracy in organizations. They also aim for consensus instead of voting, Circle thinking instead of Box. They support involving more people, evoking more honesty, eliciting more authenticity, and developing people to be their best. These methods sometimes involve randomly selected groups of people, presentations by these groups, and transformational dialogue. But the Wisdom Council is fundamentally different because it shifts the underlying structure of the system (See Chart #7).

The Wisdom Council
Changes the System

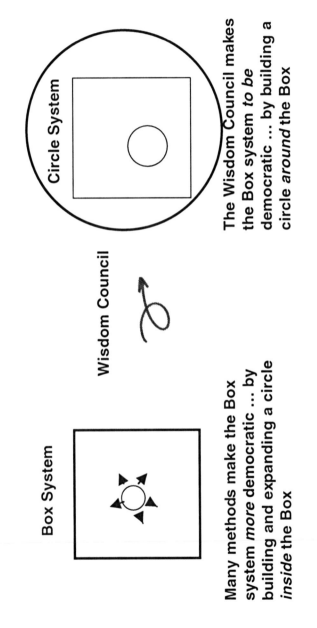

Box System

Many methods make the Box system *more democratic* ... by building and expanding a circle *inside* the Box

Wisdom Council

Circle System

The Wisdom Council makes the Box system *to be* democratic ... by building a circle *around* the Box

Chart #7

The other approaches aim to make the system *more* democratic, involving more people and influencing more decisions. But the Wisdom Council aims to make the system *be* democratic, where all participate in society's choices. The other approaches are dependent on some higher authority, like Congress, the management of the company, a powerful elite, or some sponsoring agency, to ultimately be in charge. Symbolically, the Wisdom Council *is* in charge. It is all of us deciding together what is important, what to work on, and what actions to take.

With the Wisdom Council in place, these other approaches dramatically improve their effectiveness. With it, the system supports rather than resists these democratic methods. Let's examine six alternative approaches to enhancing democracy, along with some examples of each.

1) Keeping the lines of communication open
• *Freedom of information* — Crucial to involving people is to stop keeping secrets from them. In some corporations, there is a movement to open the books and let employees know the full situation. Investigative reporters help bring out hidden information, as have laws to assure that government is truthful. The Freedom of Information Act is one example.

• *Assuring information accuracy* — Democracy is not possible if the public receives distorted information. This has become a severe problem with today's corporate-dominated media. Some prominent reforms are to create independent media sources or to organize independent news coverage.

2) Listening to the people
• *Polls* — To take a poll is to ask carefully prepared questions of a subgroup of a large population. The results are tabulated and analyzed, so that whoever is in charge can infer how all the people of the system would respond if asked the same questions. The sample size must be large enough to be

"statistically significant" so that these inferences have meaning.

• *Focus groups* — A focus group is a smaller, carefully selected group of people from a targeted population, brought together to talk about issues that interest some client. Corporations often use them to target their advertising. A facilitator asks questions of the group to determine what these people really think.

A combination of polling and focus groups is what Jim Fishkin at the University of Texas calls a "deliberative poll." Here, a large group of citizens is randomly selected and then surveyed to determine their opinions on particular questions. Then they are brought together to listen to experts and to talk among themselves in small groups. They are surveyed again to see how their views have changed.

• *Advisory panels* — Citizen advisory panels are usually appointed, but they can be randomly selected, to study issues and to recommend actions. Denmark uses "technology panels," for instance, in which groups of fifteen or so people are randomly selected and convened for a few months to study, understand, and report back on difficult technical issues. For example, panel members interview experts on genetic engineering, become knowledgeable, and then are facilitated to make policy recommendations.

• *Juries* — Here, a random selection of people is taken from a large population to reflect "the people." In our legal system, lawyers screen this group to seek out twelve who are likely to judge in favor of their client. The jury is then provided with a specific topic and a limited number of possible conclusions, like guilty and not guilty. The final result must be unanimous.

Since 1974, the Jefferson Center, founded by Ned Crosby, has organized and conducted what he calls "Citizens Juries" (see www.jefferson-center.org). They use a stratified random sampling process in terms of age, education, gender, geographic location, race, and sometimes political attitude to create a group that proportionately reflects the makeup of society. Each twenty-four person Citizens Jury has a sponsor, like a school district or governmental agency, who provides the topic. The Jury is provided with balanced expert viewpoints and a moderator to help the members ask questions, deliberate among themselves, and then vote. The hope is that there will be enough media coverage for the general citizenry to take an interest in the results.

Currently, Ned and his wife, Pat Benn, are working on a specific application of the Citizens Jury in Washington State. They suggest using Citizens Juries to evaluate proposed state initiatives before each general election and to report their conclusions in the official voters' guide.

3) Improving and educating people

• *Higher consciousness* — A favorite solution to all problems for many people is education, a particular faith, or higher consciousness. Randy Schutt, in his book, *Inciting Democracy: A Practical Proposal for Creating a Good Society*, says, " . . . the only viable way to bring about fundamental progressive change is to educate and transform every person in society so they can all then democratically choose to create a good society."

• *Basic education* — Teaching people to read and write, or to know more about democracy, collaboration, history, etc., is also necessary to improving democracy. Efforts in this direction include classes in schools, educational television, and adult programs.

4) Generating involvement

• *Promoting civil society* — Our democracy is often said to rest on a three-legged stool: government, the free market, and civil society. One strategy for improving democracy is to enhance civil society by encouraging and celebrating citizen involvement in public issues. The Giraffe Project, for instance, recognizes those who "stick their necks out." Or, corporations might sponsor company picnics or celebrations to build company spirit.

• *Generating dialogue* — A straightforward way to get people more involved is to encourage people to gather in local groups and be thoughtful on issues. In one free-wheeling form, Vicki Robin, co-author of *Your Money or Your Life*, encourages "conversation cafes." Other strategies, like the Public Conversations Project or the National Issues Forums, provide booklets on hot topics and training for group leaders.

• *Large group conferences* — One way to involve more people is to gather them together in ever larger groups. In small New England communities, sometimes the whole town can meet in one room for town hall meetings, addressing, debating, and voting on one issue at a time. Another example is what inventor Owen Harrison calls "Open Space" meetings, allowing hundreds to gather in a self-organizing format. Usually a theme or issue draws them together. Individuals stand up, one at a time, to suggest a specific subtopic they are interested in and to specify a place for people to talk about it. Through these small groups, large collections of people can jointly plan big projects and even reach joint conclusions.

"Future search" events are another example of generating more involvement that is often used by organizations. Here, sixty or more carefully selected people from different areas of an organization are brought together for a few days. They celebrate their shared history and determine a vision of a preferred future to motivate everyone.

In another large-group process, the Pew Charitable Trusts sponsored meetings of six hundred or more in a number of different cities around the country. These meetings combined small groups, experts, and high technology to address topics like Social Security. After participants listened to experts, they met in small facilitated groups, put their comments into computers that were linked together, and then watched as their votes are tallied on big screens. Then these conversations were linked via the Internet. This process had an empowering effect on those privileged to attend and this spirit can spread to affect many more people.

5) Improving the leadership

• *Replacing the leaders* — Often, the fastest way to generate participation and involvement among people in an organization is to elect or get a new leader who understands consensus and has facilitative skills. As Carol Pearson, Ph.D., author of *The Hero Within*, said in an interview: "What we expect from a leader now is . . . less a great person—unlike us—and more a facilitator of consensus."

• *Educating the leaders* — It is also possible to educate leaders to become more facilitative. Consultant Mark Gerzon, for example, organized congressional retreats where the members of Congress got to know one another outside of the normal debates and party politics. They met each another's families and engaged in informal talking. The hope was that, by knowing one another better, they would be more collaborative as leaders.

6) Putting "the people" in charge

• *Direct democracy* — It seems logical that an increased use of citizen initiatives, the election of judges, and direct voting on issues will bring more citizen involvement and greater democracy. But while these steps have a certain appeal, in practice they are often a lessening of democracy. Without a structured, thoughtful dialogue among the people, these processes are easily swayed by well-organized special interest groups, and ultimate decisions often go against the public good.

• *Delegation and self-managing teams* — Corporations and government agencies are discovering the value of self-managing teams where employees make important decisions. It is natural in our republic for people to volunteer, to get involved, and to independently act to make things better.

The above strategies and procedures are well tested to enhance the democratic spirit. But, even when used all together, they cannot transform a large system from Box to a Circle. The Wisdom Council is the missing ingredient, which makes this shift and that makes these other approaches more effective.

— 7 —

The Citizens Amendment

*We have outgrown our political system. We must face
this frankly. We had, first, government by law, second,
government by parties and big business, and all the
time some sort of fiction of 'consent of the governed'
which we said meant democracy. But we have never
had government by the people. The third step is to be
the development of machinery by which the
fundamental ideas of the people can be got at and
embodied; further, by which we can grow
fundamental ideas; further still, by which we can
prepare the soil in which fundamental ideas can grow.*

Mary Parker Follett, *The New State—Group
Organization: The Solution of Popular Government
(1918)*

*T*rue democracy, or something very close to it, is
practical and possible. We need a society where
people are working together, thinking creatively, and
seeking what is best for all. We need to define our civilization "not by

the things which our technology makes possible, but by which possibilities we choose." (Tom Abate in *Timeline*, July/August 2001.) This kind of democracy requires a change to the structure of our system.

The Proposed U.S. Constitutional Amendment

The Citizens Amendment is presented below, followed by an explanation of the important phrases. It is worded so that all twelve features of the Wisdom Council are in place.

The Citizens Amendment to the U.S. Constitution

Section 1: Not less than once each year, twenty-four registered voters shall be randomly selected to meet for one week. Those who attend all sessions shall form a Citizens Wisdom Council whose unanimous views are termed "Statements of the People." Immediately following their meeting, the Wisdom Council will present their Statements back to the people.

Section 2: At the discretion of a majority of its members, Wisdom Council meetings are public, so that all citizens may participate vicariously.

Section 3: Meeting facilitators shall be provided to ensure that the conversation in the Citizens Wisdom Council is collaborative, open-minded, and creative, and that the viewpoint of every Council member is heard and respected. Facilitators shall not express their views on matters before the Wisdom Council, nor allow their views to influence the Council's decisions.

Section 4: A Support Committee comprised of twelve previous Wisdom Council members shall ensure the integrity of the process, provide for capable facilitation and, when requested, arrange for elected officials or experts to contribute their views.

Section 5: A majority vote of the Wisdom Council members may decide procedural issues.

Expanding the Meanings

• *Section 1* ensures that Statements of the People are created and presented annually.

"... each year ..."

The Wisdom Council must be a regular event. Once a year is adequate to maintain the dialogue and ensure the attention of most Americans. But it may be that more frequent Wisdom Councils are desired. The meetings can be coordinated with the president's State of the Union message or at the beginning of a new Congress. Or they can be scheduled around the Fourth of July or some other historically significant date.

"... twenty-four ..."

The Wisdom Council is a symbol, not a poll. Therefore, it can comprise any number of people. The concept of "statistical significance" has no relevance.

The group need only be large enough so that many different viewpoints are heard and so that most people in the larger audience will identify with at least one member. It needs to be a "small group process" so people get to know one another, talk transformationally, and have the opportunity to reach true consensus. Here, a target of twenty-four is suggested because it is the largest workable "small group process." As trust develops, a lower number such as sixteen, or even twelve, may be used.

"... randomly selected ..."

Random selection establishes a microcosm of the people, as opposed to a representative body. While representatives must always keep in mind the views of their constituents, there is no constituency for those in a microcosm. Each person is free to fully engage topics, learning and growing in perspective.

" . . . registered voters . . . "

To create a random sample, we must draw from some predefined population. Currently, the official decision-making population is the pool of registered voters, so that is what has been written here. In the future, however, We the People may want to enlarge this pool to include others—high school age youth, U.S. residents who are not citizens, former prison inmates who have served their time, but who have lost the right to vote, or even current inmates.

" . . . meet for one week. "

One week is more than adequate to develop consensus on a theme or crucial issue. In addition, the time is short enough that most people can afford to take a week away from their lives without dramatic effects. Congress may want to mandate that employers make this time available in the same way they currently respect time off for training in the National Guard.

This length of time needs to be short enough that members can be plucked from their normal lives and returned before they become celebrities. This way, the Wisdom Council is always comprised of ordinary people.

"Those who attend all sessions . . . "

It is important that all members of the Citizens Wisdom Council participate fully in all meetings. Those who miss sessions cannot progress at the same rate as others, would not share the same level of commitment to decisions, and would limit the group's progress by their absence.

Upon selection, each person must commit to attending all sessions. Only those who actually attend all sessions are considered members of the Wisdom Council.

". . . form a Citizens Wisdom Council . . ."

The Citizens Wisdom Council is unique. Unlike a jury, a focus group, or an advisory board, there is no higher authority to select the topics or frame them. A jury, for example, is assigned a specific task and given a limited number of conclusions from which to choose. An advisory board merely offers advice.

The Wisdom Council, on the other hand, symbolically acts with the authority of the People. This group picks the issues, frames them, and then determines its own conclusions.

". . . unanimous views . . ."

The Wisdom Council seeks to achieve true consensus, beyond unanimity, where every member and every citizen *supports* each conclusion. In this case, the requirement for unanimity helps the group achieve consensus.

". . . Statements of the People."

Statements of the People may take any number of forms. One might be phrased as a question, "How can we build more fairness into society?" This directs attention to, and sparks thinking on, this issue. Or, it may be a recommendation like, "We believe a Citizens Panel should explore the various options for improved health care and make a recommendation to Congress or next year's Wisdom Council." The Citizens Wisdom Council can empower a Citizens Panel far more effectively than can any other entity—Congress, government agency, or non-profit organization. In this way, the Citizens Wisdom Council can effectively extend its life throughout the year and simultaneously amplify the many already-existing voices of the people that are currently muted in volume.

Also, Statements might take a new path altogether. Wisdom Councils might create a sculpture, poem, song, or some other type of communication besides language. After all, when we change the basis of society from a set of agreements to a heart-felt conversation, it is likely that our modes of communication will expand.

"*. . . will present their Statements . . .*"

One of the primary purposes of the Citizens Wisdom Council is to help all of us reflect on the issues of the day and engage in dialogue about them. Hopefully, a new national ceremony will be created around the presentation of these Statements, and people will gather in homes, churches, and community centers to talk about them. Thoughts and ideas will then evolve throughout the year.

• *Section 2* provides a way for the entire nation to identify with the people on the Wisdom Council and to participate vicariously.

"*. . . meetings are public . . .*"

As a symbol of We the People, Council members are the ultimate authority. So it is up to them whether or not to televise their daily deliberations. Certain sessions may need to be private so members can speak freely. Then the Wisdom Council won't allow cameras. But other times, the Wisdom Council may wish to amplify its impact by allowing cameras. This section of the Amendment encourages Council members to televise the conversations.

• *Section 3* ensures that the Wisdom Council meetings will be transformational rather than transactional, Choice-creating not decision-making.

"*Meeting facilitators . . . collaborative, open-minded, and creative . . .*"

The quality of the Wisdom Council's conversation is more important than who is chosen to serve on it. If the process is creative and collaborative, individual differences become assets rather than liabilities, and a kind of "universal wisdom" emerges. A key way in which the spirit of Choice-creating can be established is through effective, Dynamic Facilitation.

• *Section 4* ensures that the Wisdom Council has adequate support during its operation.

"A Support Committee . . ."

The Support Committee makes all necessary arrangements for the meetings, works out the details of the lottery, and selects appropriate facilitators and locations. They also prepare information to orient new Wisdom Council members and to provide organizational support. If the Wisdom Council asks to speak to the president, for example, the Support Committee would make the arrangements.

" *. . . comprised of twelve previous Wisdom Council members . . ."*

Those who served on previous Wisdom Councils will have experience with the process, will be independent, and will be known and trusted by the public at large. Twelve is a good-sized work group for reaching decisions on planning details.

• *Section 5* ensures that the Wisdom Council can efficiently manage itself.

" *. . . procedural issues."*

As well as addressing important societal issues, the Wisdom Council must also manage itself. Some of these decisions can include replacing the facilitator, selecting evening activities, deciding whether or not to televise the sessions, or asking to consult with experts. The group should seek consensus on these more mundane issues, but if they want, they can decide them with a vote.

A Vision of Implementation

Like the rest of the Constitution, the Amendment contains few details about implementation. Much is left to Congress, their designates, and the people selected to be on Wisdom Councils to establish and adjust the process. However, I have made some guesses as to how things will turn out.

Chartering the Wisdom Council

This idea must reach the mainstream of American political discourse. It needs to be debated on television talk shows where political pundits dissect it. Students in high schools and colleges will need to consider the idea in their classes and write term papers discussing its merits. A number of high schools will try it out, setting up Wisdom Councils and experiencing the process firsthand. Various city and county governments will attempt them, as will unions and some corporations. Certainly, too, a national magazine or a large, non-profit organization will hold a national trial of the idea so that, in short order, many people will experience and understand it.

In the end (probably in response to some crisis), Congress will take up the Amendment as a legitimate proposal. Committees in the Senate and House of Representatives will hold hearings and vote on its adoption. The proposed Amendment will pass by a two-thirds majority in both houses, and will move on to the state legislatures where three-fourths of them will eventually ratify it as an Amendment.

Ordinarily, amending the Constitution is a huge hurdle. Only twenty-seven times has it been done, and the first ten were the Bill of Rights. But this particular Amendment will have an advantage. By the time it's proposed, it will have already been adopted by many organizations, so that many people will appreciate its merits. They will understand the substantial difference between Choice-creating, which the Wisdom Council promotes, and decision-making, which our current system demands. And the more we face difficult issues, the more people will long for thoughtful, creative deliberation rather than political bickering. Furthermore, for society as a whole, there is no downside to this Amendment. So it is safe to adopt.

Assembling the Wisdom Council Members

Early in the year, every registered voter would be assigned a number from 1 to *n*, where n is the total number of registered voters. A few weeks later, a computer sampling program would generate ten thousand random numbers between 1 and *n*. These numbers would be published in newspapers and posted on the Internet. All those selected would receive a letter congratulating them for being part of the draw and be assigned a new number from 1 to 10,000. At this point, those who cannot or do not wish to participate will remove their names from the list.

Then a "high hoopla" lottery device with bouncing ping pong balls will select twenty-four willing participants from the sample of ten thousand. Although this ceremony would be nationally televised, the names of the selected people would not be released immediately.

Staff members from the Support Committee would contact each new Wisdom Council member to inform them of their selection and encourage them to attend. If at this point, some are unable or unwilling to participate in all sessions, they would not be replaced. The staff makes travel plans, arranges for stipends and expenses, and provides information about previous Statements of the People.

Wisdom Council Meetings

Wisdom Councils will meet after elections, as newly elected representatives settle into office. This makes a new president, for example, available to meet with the Wisdom Council.

Wisdom Council meetings are held in a retreat environment, isolated from the general media. The first evening, as members arrive, they begin to get to know one another and get accustomed to their new situation and living arrangements.

The next morning, the group begins work by deciding how they want to govern themselves. For instance, members may wish to limit the use of alcohol or to avoid communicating with outsiders during the week. Although consensus is sought, voting may be used during this portion of the meeting.

Once procedural matters are settled, the Dynamic Facilitator reminds the Council members that it is their meeting, asks, "What are some of the issues you might like to address?" and helps the group develop a list. The Congress, the president, various newspaper editorials, and nonprofit groups will have suggested topics, but in the end, it is the Wisdom Council that decides.

Then the facilitator helps the Wisdom Council identify which issue to work on first, and facilitates the conversation. In particular, he or she ensures that everyone is protected from judgment and orients the group to Choice-creating.

During the meetings, the Wisdom Council may wish to hear from experts, or to speak with the president or congressional leaders. Such consultation is not essential, but the group may want this. All aspects of the Wisdom Council are voluntary, so they can only request.

At the close of each day's meeting, the Wisdom Council will assess how things are going. Members will review the performance of the facilitators and, if changes are necessary, direct the Support Committee to make them.

The Presentation

The results of the meetings are official Statements of the People, along with personal stories of how these Statements came to be. The Statements will be expressions of heartfelt values, questions, shared challenges, or specific recommended actions. They will be directed to U.S. citizens, legislators, corporations, or to the people of other countries and the world. Some will be long, some short. The door is wide open for advances in the art of self-governance.

At the end of the week, immediately after the meetings are concluded, there is a short presentation to the people of the United States and the world. It should last less than two hours, with some time for individuals to speak personally about the experience.

Members of Congress and key government officials will attend the presentation.

Follow-up dialogues

Right after the presentation ceremony, people will gather in community halls, churches, and homes to consider the ideas. These gatherings are not specifically mandated in the Amendment, but will arise naturally through the sponsorship of local government, non-profit organizations, churches, and individuals. Electronic news groups, websites, and chat rooms will also be established, linked and made available for anyone to make additional points and to see what others are saying. Those who disagree with the Wisdom Council's conclusions will be the most motivated to speak out. They will write letters to the editor and tell their friends. Since their views will be most unusual, people will be curious and the media will be drawn to hear and publicize them.

The ongoing national dialogue will involve everyone. It will continue to reverberate throughout the year in talk shows, newspaper columns, Internet chat groups, schools, and other venues. Points made by participants will be refined and expanded so that in the next year, when the new Wisdom Council meets, it will reach even better conclusions. Over time, the whole country will learn and grow, as though all of us were participants in a huge, "small-group" conversation.

Selecting the Support Committee

Wisdom Council members who are interested in serving on the Support Committee will nominate themselves. Then, in a secret ballot, their nomination will be seconded by a majority vote of Wisdom Council members. From those nominated and seconded, four will be *randomly* selected to serve for a three-year term. During the initial years when the process is just beginning, randomly selected members of the House of Representatives will fill the empty positions.

These are my guesses. In the end, this process is about trusting ordinary people, knowing that they will rise to the occasion and demonstrate that they are capable of directing how things will go. It's the basic idea of democracy.

– 8 –

Models of Change / Levels of Thinking

We can not solve our problems with the same level of thinking that created them.

Albert Einstein

*W*hen people first asked me, "What value would the Amendment bring?" I often found myself talking past them instead of with them. They had a particular image in mind of how change should happen that was different than the perspective I was assuming. In this chapter I'll briefly describe five different perspectives on change. This sets the stage for the rest of the book, where we take up each one, like putting on different pairs of glasses, and examine how the Amendment would affect things.

I'd like to start this exploration by distinguishing between two opposite approaches to change: *managing* and *facilitating*. To manage change is to assume that you are dealing with dead matter rather than living beings. It requires the skills of control and planning to tame chaos and build something that works. To facilitate change is to assume that you are dealing with living systems that grow and change by themselves. You do what is needed to evoke and enhance this natural self-organizing process.

You don't "build" a garden, for instance, by shaping objects to look like leaves, flowers, and stems, glue and paint them, and deposit them in the dirt. There is managing to do in a garden, but, ultimately, you must facilitate the natural growth of the plants.

The five perspectives on change are different blends of these two opposites, managing and facilitating. The Amendment shifts us to the Circle system, which is most facilitative. Certainly, there is some managing involved, but democracy, trust, and the spirit of community are fundamentally self-organizing phenomena. They are living processes that flow bottom up, not top down. They aren't about government; they are about people.

Self-organizing Change

When we approach any task as though it can be managed and controlled, we are operating from an eighteenth century version of common sense, exemplified by Newton's Laws of Physics. These say that an object at rest, or at a constant momentum, will remain so unless some outside force is applied. Nothing changes unless something or someone *makes* it change. Adopting this perspective helps us gain control over bad situations and helps us build complex machines.

But we now know through modern sciences like quantum mechanics, biology, and cosmology, that there are no "objects" in the natural universe, that every "thing" is self-organizing. From the Big Bang forward, the cosmos has been growing in complexity through self-organizing change. From quantum mechanics and $E=mc^2$, we know that the smallest bits of matter aren't dead, but have potential for spontaneous, uncaused change. So the idea of managed change is a human invention, inconsistent with nature, which can be applied only occasionally.

The eighteenth century Box system, however, emphasizes managing change. It encourages us to use the methods of control, even for living systems like meetings, the environment, and our children, rather than supporting their capacity for self-organization. This is true, even though in our hearts we know that what is most meaningful in life—like falling in love, giving birth, being creative, and building community—are necessarily self-organizing, and can't be managed. As biologist Elisabet Sahtauris said, "The fact is that you can't turn living things into machinery. You can try to force them to behave like machinery but they will not be machinery. That is exactly why our economists can't predict anymore and our politics is falling apart. We don't understand them as unhealthy living systems. We're trying to fix them like machines. It's very different to cure a person than to fix a machine." (*Insight and Outlook*, with Scott London)

There are times when it is appropriate to manage change, but we cannot get so absorbed in this approach that we lose track of the way nature really works. If we do, we will face resistance and breakdowns. This is what happens when children rebel as teenagers, and what happened when the colonists of North America rebelled against Great Britain in 1776.

As a society, we must shift from trying to control change to facilitating it. The prospect of this shift offers great hope for us in addressing and solving all of today's big issues, like the threat of global warming, the loss of soils, water, and the ozone layer, the corporate takeover of democracy, etc. With it, we stop working so hard at jobs we "have to" do, stop aiming so much at money, and begin following our natural instincts to help others and to help society.

Levels of Capability & Self-organization

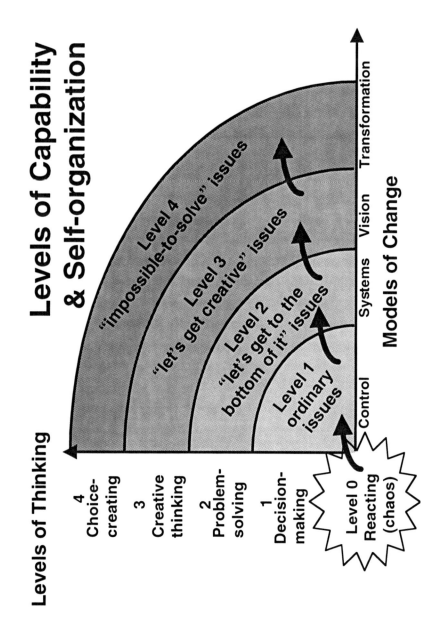

Levels of Thinking

4
Choice-creating

3
Creative thinking

2
Problem-solving

1
Decision-making

Level 0
Reacting
(chaos)

Level 4
"impossible-to-solve" issues

Level 3
"let's get creative" issues

Level 2
"let's get to the bottom of it" issues

Level 1
ordinary issues

Models of Change

Control   Systems   Vision   Transformation

Chart #8

Levels of Self-organizing Change

Self-organizing change is at the heart of democracy. It is the idea that ordinary people can responsibly manage themselves, both individually and as a society. Of course, the Founders made a giant shift in this direction with the advent of the U.S. Constitution. It was put in place with the consent of the governed; it established free elections; and it assured individual freedoms. But without a legitimate, ongoing We the People, it morphed into the Box system which is, ultimately, control-oriented. There is no king to exert arbitrary authority from the top, but he has been replaced by a constitutional mechanism, which exerts top-down control. Now, we must take another step forward on the path to increased self-organization and greater democracy.

Shifting a system to become more self-organizing is not just a matter of letting go. That would bring chaos. But so will adhering to the methods of control. Better is to keep the mechanisms of control in place while we facilitate more self-organization. Then, as people become empowered, they can use their new power to responsibly take charge.

Chart #8 illustrates the natural progression of empowerment, steps we all go through at times. Five levels are depicted, each of which, except for the first, has a viewpoint of how change happens and an associated style of thinking.

Four of the levels are particularly important because they represent wholly different perspectives from which to view the Citizens Amendment, to understand how it would work, and to "get" its significance. The rest of the book is organized around these viewpoints.

Level 0: Reacting (Chaos)

Level 0 is a pre-thinking stage, "reacting." There is no model of change, nor can we say that there is any real thinking, because people in this state of mind are just responding to stimuli. Change happens *to* them, not the other way around. They do the best they can, moving away from what is threatening, toward what is pleasing.

All of us know this stage of development because it happens when we are placed in a new context, when we are not feeling well, when we've received bad news, or when we just don't know what is going on. Our environment is in control of us. It is mostly from this level that the voting public currently operates, lurching from one position to another, depending on the dictates of the media and the mood of the situation.

Some young people operate from here as well. Those who have had either too little or too much structure in their lives often get stuck at Level 0 once they are independent. They lose their way, get involved in drugs or other negative influences, and just do whatever comes to them in the moment.

For these young people, a successful transition from this state to Level 1, the beginning of thinking, often comes in the form of imposed discipline. Military boot camp, for instance, can be a powerful turn-around. In the military, they are given a specific set of "right" answers—what to say, how to dress, when to get up, etc. This discipline, this clear pattern of right and wrong, can often help these people start making more conscious decisions.

Someone operating at Level 0 might ask about the Amendment, "What would it do for me today?"

Level 1 Thinking: Decision-making

The shift to Level 1 means seizing more control over the environment. It can begin when we start to notice patterns in what is happening, and develop routines or norms around them. Sometimes an expert will teach us the ropes, or we learn from past experience.

Level 1 thinking is "decision-making"—evaluating options and selecting them according to a particular description of goodness. A manager, for instance, uses this level of thinking when she seeks to improve her organization by evaluating the people in it, one by one according to set standards, rewarding those who are doing well, and improving or getting rid of the bad performers. It is a model of change which assumes that the organization is composed of separate individuals who can be evaluated independently.

This style of thinking is well suited to the Box structure because it assumes we can make decisions through codified procedures. It's how we structured our judicial system, for example, to apply the letter of the law rather than the spirit of the law. Such decision-making approaches can be efficient for simple decisions, but often fail to account for the real needs of people or generate real commitment to decisions.

A person using Level 1 thinking might ask about the Citizens Amendment, "Would the Amendment help us to enact better laws? And, since it doesn't have any coercive authority, how would it help us overcome the power of special interests?" *Chapter 9 — Power and Control (Level 1)* answers these questions.

Level 2 Thinking: Problem-solving

Life is more complex than Level 1 thinking allows and, at some point, we start to notice that our attempts to gain more control actually reduce it. For instance, as we add more and more people to prisons in an attempt to increase personal security, we actually diminish it. Prisons teach criminal behaviors to nonviolent offenders, disrupt families and their earnings, build resentment among the poor people and racial minorities who disproportionately occupy the jails, undermine democracy by denying the vote to those who have served their time, generate exorbitant expenses that are borne by the general population, and do not help victims get restitution.

The transition to Level 2 thinking, "problem-solving," begins by acknowledging these unintended consequences and letting go of the idea that black and white answers will always work. It is a step away from the idea that there is one right answer and a step toward carefully considering many ideas, discussing reasons for and against each one.

Level 2 is the ideal mode of thinking in our Box system, sometimes called "deliberative democracy." It is when we rely on evaluative, critical thinking skills, along with discussion and debate, to rationally determine the "best" answers. It assumes a systems model of change, where we recognize that the apparent problem may just be a symptom of some deeper issue, and we seek to understand what is really happening.

The difference between Level 1 and Level 2 can be demonstrated by a visit to a hardware store. If you have a simple clear problem, Level 1 thinking is most appropriate. The clerk just directs you to the appropriate product on the shelf. At other times though, you may not fully understand the problem you are facing. You want a Level 2 thinker, someone who has experience with this kind of problem, to help you think it through.

The kind of question that a Level 2 thinker might ask about the Citizens Amendment is, "Would it adjust our system so that we are more deliberative, collaborative, and that we make smarter decisions?" *Chapter 10 — Reshaping the System (Level 2)* addresses this question.

Level 3 Thinking: Creative Thinking

When problems get even more complex, when issues seem impossible to solve, we may need to let go of control even more. The next "letting go" is to abandon the idea that our conscious minds can do it all and invite our unconscious minds to help. Level 3 is "creative thinking."

We might establish and articulate a vision of what we want. Sometimes that's enough to manifest it. In other cases, brainstorming, lateral thinking, positive affirmations, and spiritual meditation can be used. Each calls forth more self-organizing change.

With brainstorming, for instance, we imagine a problem and then allow our creative minds to self-organize many ideas. We don't evaluate them, but just get out of the way and let them come. Surprisingly, after a time, we realize that many of these ideas, which at first seemed foolish, have exciting potential.

All of us open ourselves to Level 3 thinking when we dream, stand in the shower, play music, or sit quietly. In the words of Albert Einstein, " . . . the gift of fantasy has meant more to me than my talent for absorbing positive knowledge." Corporations have recognized this value and seek to foster it in employees. They often gather them together, for example, to develop a company vision, fashion a mission statement, or formulate shared values. Just holding meetings and developing these statements, whether specific actions are taken or not, help raise the organization's level of capability for self-organizing change.

A question about the Citizens Amendment from someone thinking at Level 3 might be, "Would it help us establish a shared vision and become more creative?" *Chapter 11 — Creating Shared Vision (Level 3)* will address this.

Level 4 Thinking: Choice-creating

Level 3 also has its limits. Some issues are so impossible-seeming that a miracle is needed or, at least, a transformation. In a crisis, a person can feel powerless and emotionally overwhelmed. But these issues can be solved with another "letting go," one that evokes creativity of both head and heart, as well as logic. Level 4 is Choice-creating.

Choice-creating can happen naturally when we care deeply about a problem that seems impossible to solve. The trick is to stay both caring and creative, even to the point of letting go of who we think we are. Then we open a door to the possibility of personal transformation.

Stories about how transformation happens are the substance of our favorite myths. The story of *Star Wars*, for instance, is a modern dragon myth where a heroic figure faces and defeats the evil Darth Vader and the Death Star. Vader is all powerful at first, and can easily outfight our hero, Luke Skywalker. Luke goes through all the levels we've been talking about. First, he discovers his aunt and uncle murdered, and decides to go after the murderers. Then he starts to understand more about what he's up against, and works with others to defeat the Empire.

In time, Luke gains a vision of what he might become, a Jedi knight. He isn't very good at following his master's instructions and struggles with it, but when he eventually faces the ultimate test, one person against the Death Star, it isn't his fighting skills that save him. To reach the fourth and uppermost level, he must let go of those and "trust the force." Only then can a miracle happen, only then can he do the impossible and succeed—becoming a different person in the process. Later, he faces another crisis in fighting Darth Vader. Again, all seems lost. But when he trusts the force, Luke not only survives but a transformation begins in Darth Vader as he feels the stirring of compassion for his long-lost son. In this instance, both are transformed to father and son, and a new "Kingdom" is born.

In a more down-to-earth example, M. Scott Peck describes how this transformational process is *required* to build community. In his book, *A Different Drum: Community and Peacemaking*, he says that people in the groups he works with start out thinking of themselves as already being a community. After a while, differences are discovered and people try to fix each other, but this only makes things worse. Good feelings deteriorate and the "community" eventually faces a crisis where it may dissolve completely. Peck sees this deterioration as part of a healthy process. He warns that if an authoritarian leader were to impose order on the chaos at this stage, the chance for achieving true community would be lost.

What happens next is "emptiness," where people let go of their efforts to fix others and they accept their inability to "build" community. Paradoxically, this seeming failure makes room for transformation, for true community to self-organize.

Wise prophets throughout history have described this "letting go and trusting the force" process. Jesus described it as a paradox, "Whosoever shall seek to save his life shall lose it; and whosoever shall lose his life shall save it." (Luke: 17:33) Lao Tzu, from the fifth century, BCE said, "When I let go of what I am, I become what I might be."

This final level of self-organizing change can work for society as well as for people. It is the creation of a "wise democracy," where all of us face and solve the big issues together, using both creativity and reason. As Nietsche said, "A necessary condition for a miracle is to be at an impasse that only a miracle can resolve."

Someone thinking at this level might ask, "Will the Citizens Amendment facilitate us as a society, to address our most crucial issues creatively, collaboratively, and with wisdom?" There are three chapters on how it would do this: *Chapter 12 — "Turning On" Our System, Chapter 13 — Choosing to BE,* and *Chapter 14 — Changing Our Mythology.*

Part III

CHANGING SOCIETY

Let us put our heads together and see what life we will make for our children.

Tatanka Iotanka (Sitting Bull, Lakota Leader)

— 9 —

Power and Control (Level 1)

We're not going to defeat or overthrow, or even abandon the corporatist structure in spite of its failures. This is a system that continually grows stronger while the society it controls grows weaker. It's therefore a matter of inserting the citizen, as citizen, into the system in whatever way we can.

John Ralston Saul, *The Unconscious Civilization*

I was once trying to explain to an environmental activist how the Citizens Amendment would help her work. I was describing how it would change the quality of our political conversation, how it would generate systemic thinking, transform people's attitudes, and how it would encourage Choice-creating instead of decision-making. To me, these were crucial changes. But she was waging a war against special interests and didn't want to hear my ideas for ending the war. She wanted to know how the Amendment would help her win. I was enamored with Level 4 change, while she was focused on Level 1 change, how the people could gain enough power within the system to change the laws. The more I talked, the more frustrated she became. Interrupting, she asked, "So, when would the smokestacks come down?"

Politics is a Battle

The Citizens Amendment would help her efforts because it redistributes power. It creates a new institution that gives a poor person just as much say as one who is wealthy. It gives the voice of Native Americans, small business owners, retired people, smokers, single moms, non-voters, environmentalists, lawyers, welfare recipients, young people, and all hyphenated-Americans a new opportunity to speak and be heard in proportion to the number of their population in the pool of registered voters. For example, *over time* there would be just as many women chosen for Wisdom Councils as men.

There is another important power shift in the Amendment—from special interests to the public interest. The real battle for power in our system today is between highly-organized special interests and the poorly-organized general interest. The Amendment would de-emphasize those speaking for their own best interest and strengthen the voice of those seeking what is best for all.

Currently, corporations dominate the political agenda and shape how we think. By controlling the mass media, they ensure that the general interest perspective gets drowned out. As William Greider says in his book, *Who Will Tell the People: The Betrayal of American Democracy*, "The present system provides no reliable mechanism to represent the people on the most important governing questions—no institution that is committed to listening to them and to speaking for them, no organization that mobilizes the potential strength of people and uses it to confront the rival power of organized money. The problem of modern democracy is rooted in its neglect of unorganized people."

To answer my activist friend's question about when the smokestacks would come down, let's consider one way this might work. First, a Wisdom Council would bring up the topic of pollution. The people on it would consider different approaches to solving it, thinking the topic through, and determining what's best. In the end, they would reach some form of consensus, maybe suggesting a different way to think about it, defining the problem, or even proposing a specific piece of legislation. Let's say they do the last. After the suggested legislation is presented to the nation as a Statement of the People, many of us would talk about this proposal in classrooms, at work, in the hallways of Congress, on the Internet, in the media, etc. Voices from all sectors of society would be heard, including corporations, environmentalists, and academia. New and even better ideas would be aired and considered. Congress might act at this point, but it would probably be better if they waited until some form of consensus emerged.

In the next Wisdom Council, the issue would arise again. One or more new Wisdom Council members would know what had happened previously. He or she would help the new group to understand the concerns expressed about last year's proposal and suggest something better. This Wisdom Council would then reach new conclusions, possibly proposing new legislation and asking Congress for action.

As it becomes clear that leadership from the people is wise and reasonable, I suspect that members of Congress would welcome, not resist it. Coming from a truly, non-partisan source, elected representatives would have a clear mandate from the people that could offset special interest pressure they receive. It would also elevate the understanding of issues among their constituents, so that the representatives can serve the public interest without suffering at the polls.

But even if Congress were to ignore the wishes of the second Wisdom Council, a third Wisdom Council could take up the matter again. If it were ever necessary, the people can enforce their will by recommending that offending elected representatives be un-elected. We must remember that the people already have ultimate power in our system. It's just that they currently don't have a way to use it intelligently. The Citizens Amendment provides them with the means to get organized and determine what is needed. If it ever came down to it, a consensus of the people can always trump Congress, the president, or even the Constitution.

Corporations Are Not Human

Two hundred-plus years ago, when the Founders designed our system, they didn't have this problem nearly as much. Then, a struggle among special interests served the general interest. But with our system growing ever more complex, especially with the advent of powerful autonomous corporations, this is no longer true.

Corporations in the United States were originally public institutions, each one rooted in a community with an owner-manager. But now, they are increasingly governed by absentee stockholders who may not even know where the corporations are located or what products they produce. The owners might be institutional investors or day traders exclusively focused on the bottom line. This focus on the numbers, and lack of concern for local communities, the environment, or morality, ensures that today's corporations serve the Game more than the people.

Most corporations do serve people and bring benefit to society. But large transnational corporations do not have this as their primary agenda. In advertisements, they are characterized as being like the people who work for them, as having the human traits of loyalty, a sense of fairness, and concern for the planet. Many have mission statements as though their ultimate aim is to serve people. And the people in the corporation may even feel and claim to be mission-driven rather than profit-driven. But actually, it is the Game that determines the real mission of large corporations. One of the most effective ways of getting the most out of people is to enlist their natural desire to do meaningful work. So they create corporate mission statements as a tool to that end.

The best corporations do good things for employees. They involve them in developing mission statements, train them, expand the benefits, and make donations to charities. The corporation might say that "People are number one" or "Service is our top priority," and for many of the employees, it is true. But at a deeper level, encouraging employee commitment to these selfless aims is a means to an end for the corporation—more profits. It's the way the system works.

These same employees are often jolted back to this reality when the company faces a crisis. A downturn in stock price, a sudden lack of customers, a union contract negotiation, the incursion of substitute products into the market, or a change in managers will often shift the situation in a way that reveals the true values of the corporation. There will be layoffs, salary cuts, plant closures, and abrupt changes in policy by the corporation that, if it were human, would be considered immoral. But the corporation is not human. Professing one set of values, while holding another, is just playing the Game. Players bluff all the time. And, of course, a corporation cannot make a bond of trust in the first place. It is a legal construct, not a person.

Corporate Priorities vs. Human Priorities

We have left many of our most important societal decisions to the Game, allowing corporate values to make those decisions instead of human values. Some of them are: Where should we spend our scarce public monies ... defense? education? roads? What kind of relationship to the environment do we want ... stewardship? exploitation? apathy? What energy sources should we develop and use ... oil? nuclear? renewable? How should we treat people who break the law ... harsh punishment? rehabilitation? banishment? What shall we do about natural resources like the human genome, the radio frequency bands, or the minerals in the land ... make them private property and have a bidding war? just give them to the corporations? keep them public? To what end shall we educate our children? ... toward helping society? to realizing their full potential? or toward getting any job that pays well?

We make these decisions by default, trusting the mechanisms of our system, rather than thinking them through and making them jointly. Not only, for instance, do defense industry contractors largely decide how much money to spend on weapons systems, but because of the threat of job loss in key political districts, they often decide how many jet planes or submarines will be built over the objections of the Pentagon. Abraham Lincoln foresaw the unfolding of this problem, when he said in a letter to (Col.) William F. Elkins, Nov. 21, 1864, " . . . I see in the near future a crisis approaching that unnerves me and causes me to tremble for the safety of my country. . . . corporations have been enthroned and an era of corruption in high places will follow, and the money power of the country will endeavor to prolong its reign by working upon the prejudices of people until all wealth is aggregated into a few hands and the Republic is destroyed. I feel at this moment more anxiety for the safety of my country than ever before, even in the midst of war. God grant that my suspicions may prove groundless."

So far, his suspicions have been borne out in ways worse than he could have imagined. Today, humans serve corporate priorities far more than corporations serve human priorities. We are even "branded" by these companies as if we were their property, being taught to strongly prefer Coke or Pepsi, for example. It is similar to branding cattle, only in our case, the brand is inside our psyches rather than on our skins. Some of the best minds in the country have been drafted to work on this and other such issues, trying to understand young people enough to change their preference for a particular blend of sugar water.

We reward this type of work with high salaries. But anyone who wants a job directly aimed at serving humanity must expect a low salary, if any at all. My wife, a psychotherapist, founded a nonprofit organization to support the creative spirit in children, for instance. Therapists met weekly with children, an hour at a time. Parents or agencies could suggest that a child participate, but since the ultimate decision was the child's, the service was free. It was a great success within the community, with a waiting list of children, as well as volunteer therapists. However, our Box system doesn't remunerate this kind of Circle work. For the staff to receive any remuneration from the state or from foundations, her organization was pressured to become Box-like; for example, to categorize a child to be "at risk," with therapeutic objectives and measures of progress. It's an odd way to organize society, around corporate values rather than human values.

The tobacco industry is one example of high rewards being achieved at the *expense* of people—and it happens on center stage while we all watch. It's been determined for many years that cigarettes are addictive and damaging to the health of both smokers and nonsmokers. Because of the addictive nature of the product, it's a highly profitable business.

Through deft political donations, subtle advertising, and threats of legal action, the industry influences members of Congress, research organizations, university professors, and even nonprofit groups to contribute to their aims. The following disclaimers are attached to various Acts of Congress:

- The Consumer Product Safety Act states: "The term 'consumer product' does not include tobacco and tobacco products.
- The Fair Packaging and Labeling Act states: " 'Consumer commodity' does not include tobacco or any tobacco product."

- The Hazardous Substances Act states: "The term 'hazardous substance' shall not apply to tobacco and tobacco products."
- The Toxic Substances Control Act states: "The term 'chemical substance' does not include tobacco or any tobacco product."

During the spring of 1998, Senator John McCain introduced a bill to force tobacco companies to pay to help stop youths from starting the habit. The bill left committee with 19 of 20 senators in favor. A month later, after the tobacco industry started spending to defeat it, the bill was dead. A barrage of television ads convinced voters that the bill was really about taxing poor people to generate money for more government bureaucracies. Phone banks were created to take calls from upset misinformed citizens, and to route them directly to Senate offices. Ads also targeted Senator McCain's conservative constituency, implying that he had become a "tax-and-spend liberal." This media campaign was a quick lesson to any elected representative about how costly it can be to choose the human interest over the corporate interest.

Even if all human beings in this scenario—customers, politicians, tobacco company employees, tobacco farmers, reporters, elected officials, and investors—preferred to act differently, little would change. That is, even if smokers want to quit, teenagers don't really want to start, tobacco employees prefer other work, farmers prefer other crops, reporters want to tell the real story, elected officials want to enact preventative legislation, and investors are willing to sacrifice profits to help eliminate this habit, the *system* would carry on. All are trapped by their addictions, whether it be to nicotine, power, a moneyed lifestyle, or the upbeat images of subtle advertising, like being sassy and cool, or a rugged outdoorsman.

This industry is just one example of many. It receives more attention than others because the damage is so obvious. But it's an indicator of how our collective decisions are driven by corporate values rather than human values. We work and live inside a system that ostensibly serves people, but more fundamentally, people serve the system.

Shaping the Humans

That corporate values drive our lives causes deep pain for many people. In my conversations with young adults and teenagers, I've found they don't want to live their lives by these values. But they want to have a normal life, too. In one videotaped conversation on local access television, I interviewed three youths who described the pressures they feel.

Our parents and their parents have built these great industries that tell us we need to buy and buy and buy and television tells us what we need to care about. And what we need to care about is getting cool shoes . . . getting a boyfriend . . . being cute and pretty . . . having clear skin and full lips and that's not true. I think what I'm most worried about is we're going to focus on what is shown to us—a farce. We're going to be shown something that is not real and we're going to take it as real.

There are campaigns that tells us not to smoke, not to drink, not to do drugs, but I think there's a lot of stuff out there that pretty much tells us we should be drinking on the weekends and doing drugs and smoking. . . . I think materialism creates insecurity. I think if you are told you have to be this perfect thing . . . if you listen to this ideal of what you should be and you aren't, it will hurt you. . . .

It just seems like something out there is trying to get us to buy everything there could possibly be, to make ourselves into

*something they want us to be. They just want to push us . . .
And I don't want to be pushed.*

*But there's no real way that we've been given to rebel
against this push because it's so faceless. You can't pinpoint
it because it's everywhere. It's society. It's our lives . . . . And
it's really hard to know what the heck you are supposed to
rebel against. So, if anybody knows, please come up to us and
tell us.*

Many people today feel that the only way they can earn a living is
to acquiesce to this pressure, putting more carbon dioxide into the air,
using more natural resources, and generally forgetting about societal
issues to focus on our own lives. We are like particles of water in a
wave. Individually, we may only move up and down on the vertical
plane—taking care of our families and working as best we can to help
others. But together we comprise a wave, relentlessly moving on a
different plane toward ends no one wants. In the process, we get
shaped by the wave more than we shape it. How we are shaped takes
many forms.

In her book, *Endangered Pleasures: In Defense of Naps, Bacon,
Martinis, Profanity, and Other Indulgences*, Barbara Holland
describes how even our concept of fun has been shaped by these
pressures: "The permissible enjoyments now are public, official and
commercially regulated, as in Disney World, casinos, shopping,
television, organized sport and rock concerts. As long as somebody
somewhere is making money out of us, we're useful to the economy,
even patriotic: we are allowed to pay admission and play in the theme
park."

The Alec Guiness movie from 1951, *The Man in the White Suit*,
illustrates another dimension to how the wave forms our world.
Guiness's character is working in the laboratory of a textile company
and invents a fabric that is brilliantly white, resists stains, and is
indestructible. At first, the owner of the corporation is excited by this

product and its competitive advantage. But gradually, it dawns on him that this product is too good. If it were to be produced, it could only be sold once. When the unions hear about the product, they are also overcome with fear about losing their jobs. At the end of the movie, everyone from both the industry and the unions, even the owner of the company, is desperate to prevent the idea from going into production.

This story is a metaphor for how the Game ultimately limits us and our creativity. It supports innovation toward the general good only to the extent that it serves the Game. In healthcare, for example, our system sponsors an apparently fast and furious competition to develop new technologies for people. But, because there is no real benefit for a company to discover a breakthrough product that is easily and cheaply obtained, like a cure for the common cold, our system resists it. Maximum profits occur when people live long lives, but are chronically dependent on expensive drugs, food additives, high-tech medical equipment, and ongoing services. It is better for our system if human health is continually at risk from carcinogens, hormone disrupters, increased radiation, viruses, genetic tampering, and assorted pollutants that require ongoing care or remedial services.

What is Real?

Obviously, to take corrective action we must know what is going on. But our primary way of knowing things, the media, is dominated by the Game. Each media conglomerate edits out what might cost them money and edits in what might earn it. Ultimately, what we hear about on the evening news, talk shows, and entertainment is put through this filter.

For example, in 1996, when Congress was giving away seventy billion dollars worth of America's digital spectrum to the media giants, the people heard very little about it. If you were a loyal viewer of your favorite network news program then, or even a show with hard-hitting investigative reporting, you might have missed it altogether.

A tale told by two experienced reporters, Jane Akre and Steve Wilson of Florida TV station WTVT, provides a good illustration of how it works. In November 1996, Akre and Wilson were hired amid great fanfare to head the station's news investigative unit. They prepared a story about Monsanto's genetically engineered recombinant bovine growth hormone (rBGH), a product that is injected into dairy cows to induce higher milk production.

Their story addressed the issue of whether or not this hormone, now in most of the milk we buy, is good for people. They raised doubts, including these points:

- Other countries (e.g., Europe and Canada) banned the sale of these milk products.
- A majority of citizens and a number of highly qualified experts are concerned about the possibility of increased incidence of cancer from drinking milk from these cows.
- The product was investigated and deemed safe for cows by the FDA, but some rBGH-treated herds are experiencing a shortened life, hoof problems, and udder infections. The investigation by the FDA of the product's effect on humans was less rigorous than the investigation of its effect on cows, because it is not given directly to humans.
- Florida supermarkets originally promised to not sell milk from treated cows until the hormone gained widespread acceptance by consumers. But they quietly backed off from these promises.
- Farmers who are not using rBGH have found it difficult to label their milk as such in the marketplace. In two cases, farmers that tried to label their milk as being free from rBGH were sued by Monsanto. And because of

industry pressure, some states have even made such labeling illegal.

- Previous Monsanto products that received government approval were later found to be dangerous, like 2-4-5-T in Agent Orange.

But the concerns Akres and Wilson raised about this product are less important than their efforts to get the information on the air. The news story was approved by station management and scheduled to air in February 1997. In the meantime, the station was sold to the Fox network, which received an ominous letter from lawyers representing Monsanto.

The story was postponed. Fox management and lawyers carefully combed the story for bias and errors and reapproved it. Again, they received a threatening letter and it was pulled. According to the reporters, the story was written at least seventy-three times. Then, barely a year after being hired, both reporters were fired. As they say on their website, (see www.bghPOXsuit.com), "We were repeatedly ordered to go forward and broadcast demonstrably inaccurate and dishonest versions of the story." For these reporters to adhere to the truth, as they saw it, meant losing their jobs, their homes, and being tied up in litigation for years.

On August 18, 2000, a Florida state court jury determined that Fox "acted intentionally and deliberately to falsify or distort the plaintiffs' news reporting on rBGH."

We the Corporations

Nothing in this chapter is about good versus evil. There are no bad guys here. The corporations are doing what they were designed to do and, because they do it well, they have great power. The solution is not to call on more sacrifices from individuals inside and outside of corporations, or for more laws, but to make a systems change.

Corporate values have become paramount because there is no voice of the people to advocate for human values.

Worse, there is now a "We the Corporations" forming to govern international trade, officially taking the Box structure to the world. For international trade to function, there needs to be one generally accepted set of values. The World Trade Organization is proposing corporate values. It is now establishing rules of the Game for the world ... and a court to enforce those rules. Because the United States is a party to the treaties establishing the WTO, the rulings of this tribunal have great power over us.

In consequence, corporate representatives are meeting in sessions behind closed doors to decide the legality of our national and local laws. For instance, this "court" has already fined the government of Canada for enforcing one of its laws, and gutted a portion of the Endangered Species Act of the United States. This new set of rules and rulings would now outlaw the kind of economic sanctions that forced South Africa to end apartheid. If We the People existed and had a voice, surely We would rise to challenge this takeover and make sure that human values were paramount over corporate values.

Turning Things Around

The Citizens Amendment establishes a way for We the People to take charge. It gives us a way to focus on one issue, develop a strategy for dealing with it, and to speak with power. For instance, if the Wisdom Council were to choose "the corporate takeover of democracy," "the lack of citizen involvement in politics," "racism," or any such topic, there would be a whole new level of public awareness, involvement, and cohesion on the topic. Further, this cohesion would command the legislative and executive branches of government to action.

That the Citizens Amendment gives We the People real power can be seen most clearly by considering its effect on the judgments of the

Supreme Court. Assume that one Wisdom Council makes Statements of the People that are "ratified" by other Wisdom Councils so that, clearly, most everyone in the nation agrees. Now, let's say that the Supreme Court hears a case in which one claimant takes a position that runs counter to these Statements, but which is consistent with the existing interpretation of the Constitution.

With developing trust in the process, the Supreme Court will ultimately be faced with a dilemma. The Constitution is the creation of We the People of the past, while Wisdom Council Statements are the views of We the People today. In time, it is likely that the standard of judgment for the Supreme Court will change. At some point, members of the Court may consider the Statements of a constitutionally sanctioned Wisdom Council to be at least as relevant a standard as current interpretations of the Founders' intent when writing the original Constitution.

Giving Corporations a Heart

Earlier, we discussed the tragedy of the commons—how competition among the "villagers" will inevitably destroy the commons. We also saw how the Citizens Amendment would overcome this by creating a shared vision, fostering a spirit of trust and community, de-emphasizing competition, and building whole-system consciousness.

But one aspect of the dilemma, which was not discussed in that chapter, is that corporations are the new encroachers on the commons. They are inherently competitive, incapable of either trust or human relationships. So even with the Citizens Amendment in place, when the limits of the commons are reached, corporations would still be structured to compete for scarce common resources rather than collaborate.

Good leadership from corporate managers like Ray Anderson, CEO of Interface Inc., a carpet manufacturer, is not enough. One day, while reading Paul Hawken's book, *Ecology of Commerce*, he realized that his company was a major polluter, a destroyer of the earth. He pledged that this would stop. He then promoted a new vision throughout his company, to become a "net non-polluter." Employees pulled together and began innovating and making substantial gains. And simultaneously, they made money at it.

One innovative step they've taken is to recognize that used carpets do not decompose in landfills. They figured out a way to overcome this problem and still make money. They now offer to take people's used carpets and reclaim them, guaranteeing that they will not be placed in a landfill.

Creative leadership like this really works, but still, the bottom line is profits. As the company gets bigger, as Wall Street gains more power over its decisions, and as the competition tightens, cost-cutting measures will undoubtedly be sought. While some of the company's efforts to be non-polluting pay for themselves, others actually cost money. I predict that, eventually, because of cost pressures, these extra efforts will be seen as unnecessary, and eliminated. That is, rather than adhering to the vision, or to human values, the company will be forced to adhere to corporate values. Employees will be hurt by this shift of emphasis. Those who are committed to the vision will feel betrayed and leave, while others will harden their hearts and adopt the values of the Game.

There are ways, however, to assure thoughtful corporate leadership even under the pressures of global capital markets. One approach is suggested by Marjorie Kelly in her book, *The Divine Right of Capital: Dethroning the Corporate Aristocracy*. She outlines ways to return to fundamental principles like, " . . . the principle that corporations must not harm the public good, that employees are part of the corporation, that wealth belongs to those who create it, and that community wealth belongs to all."

Another approach is to implement Wisdom Councils *within corporations*. With this step, employees can transform the corporate structure from a team to a community in the same way that the Citizens Amendment supports people to transform this nation. A Wisdom Council offers a way for the people of the corporation to commit themselves to human values more than to the bottom line. And it provides a way for them to communicate that commitment to one another, to customers, and to investors.

Picture yourself doing business with another person. Would you rather that person be genuinely ethical, or that they just pretended to be that way, and were really only interested in selfish advantage? Would you rather that your business relationship be a real relationship, or just a commodity exchange? Would you rather be treated like a person or as a "human resource"? Probably, you prefer real relationship and ethical dealings. Adopting a Wisdom Council inside a transnational corporation will promote this kind of business partnership, and help us all get more of the kind of business relationship we want.

With a Wisdom Council in a corporation, an authentic corporate voice is created that is far more substantial than the voice of public relations and advertising. With it, the people in corporations can genuinely be mission-driven and choose to serve the general interest. Plus, if all corporations on the commons were to adopt Wisdom Councils, there is the potential for a "community of corporations" to arise which truly can overcome the tragedy of the commons.

— 10 —

Reshaping the System (Level 2)

. . . a system is a functioning whole that cannot be divided into independent parts and remain effective.

Russell L. Ackoff

I remember watching a friend bathing her baby in the sink. The tot was enjoying herself, splashing water and playing with tub toys. But the "toy" that most caught her interest was the drain plug. She didn't recognize that it was different from the water toys. You and I can make that distinction because we can see that the drain plug is part of a system. In playing with this toy, the child eventually pulled the plug on her bath and it soon ended.

As she grows older, she will become aware of this kind of systems connection. She will come to recognize that not all objects have toy-like independence, but are interconnected. However, as a society we are like the baby, thoughtlessly toying with many different plugs, ignorant of the potential impact this may have on our happiness.

The Power of a System

One of the best illustrations of the impact of a systems viewpoint is the Red Bead Experiment of Dr. Edwards Deming, the famous consultant for whom Japan's prestigious quality award is named. In the 1980's and '90s, Dr. Deming performed this experiment for audiences around the world. He would stand in front of corporate leaders and pretend to be the manager of the White Bead Manufacturing Company. He would enlist volunteers from the audience to come on stage and be "willing workers" in his production enterprise.

The manufacturing process for Dr. Deming's pretend company required each worker to dip a paddle having fifty indentations into a large collection of beads, of which 90% were white and 10% were red. As manager of the white bead plant, Dr. Deming was concerned because his plant also produced red beads.

To howls of laughter from the audience, Dr. Deming would try a number of traditional solutions. He rewarded the workers who produced the highest percentage of white beads, and had those workers train the others in exactly how they dipped their paddles and how they shook off the excess beads. He fired the poorest performers and replaced them with new people from the audience. He held motivational rallies. He even drafted mission statements. The audience and willing workers laughed because they saw how fruitless these steps were.

The quality control problem in the White Bead Manufacturing Company was not caused by the workers, but by the system. The manager's efforts to improve the workers only made things worse, frustrating them and removing attention from the real problem. When he finished his demonstration, Dr. Deming would point his finger at the managers in his audience and emphatically tell them that they, not their workers, were responsible for quality problems in their organizations. They were most responsible for the system and the system was the true culprit. He insisted that they stop trying to fix the people and start understanding the system, so that intelligent strategies could be devised.

To solve society's problems, we must understand his point. It is the design of our system, not the people in it, that is the culprit. Yet, like the hapless manager in Deming's experiment, we are steadfast in trying to educate, legislate, motivate, and fix the people.

His finger should be pointed at us collectively because we are, or should be, the manager of our system. We are responsible for problems like the inequitable distribution of wealth, threats to the environment, political bickering, lack of citizen involvement, etc. Yet, like the manager of the White Bead Manufacturing Company, we bemoan inauthentic politicians, apathetic citizens, inept bureaucrats, greedy corporate leaders, undereducated youth, drug addicts, etc. We are like the baby in the bath water, unaware of the pivotal role that the underlying structure plays.

The Manager of a System

In a sense, We the People existed for a brief time in 1787 at the Constitutional Convention. But that group is gone. Now, there is just the system they left, in charge of itself ... and in charge of us. The design we inherited leaves us with only a minor role to play. We are supposed to be loyal subjects of the system, occasionally voting for one candidate or another, but basically trusting it to carry on by itself.

Today even the vote has largely been taken over by the system. We are usually faced with an incumbent and a challenger, where the incumbent has a huge advantage. Two bitter camps form and both candidates aim carefully crafted, often negative messages at a few swing voters. The vast majority of people and the issues they are most concerned about go largely ignored. In the end, in the Senate and House of Representatives, the incumbent is reelected over 90% of the time. Then the special interests are repaid for their campaign

Restructuring Our System

Chart #9

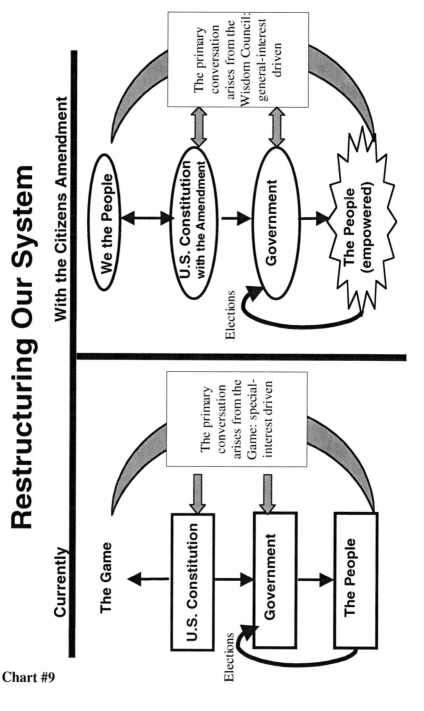

Currently

The Game

U.S. Constitution

Government

The People

Elections

The primary conversation arises from the Game: special-interest driven

With the Citizens Amendment

We the People

U.S. Constitution with the Amendment

Government

The People (empowered)

Elections

The primary conversation arises from the Wisdom Council: general-interest driven generosity with favorable legislation, while citizens turn away in disgust. There is little room in this process today for real democracy, for heartfelt talking about what's important, and for making things work for everyone.

The Citizens Amendment remedies this by providing us, the people, with a way to become We the People, and to exercise our rightful authority over the system. Chart #9 illustrates the change. On the left is how our system currently works. On the right is how it should work.

In today's hierarchy of power, the Game occupies the top position, while the people are at the bottom. The people have minimal input or involvement in ultimate decisions. But the Citizens Amendment rearranges this hierarchy and changes how it works. It facilitates and places an overarching Choice-creating conversation in top position, with all of us participating and with human values paramount.

Systems Thinking

Besides altering the structure of the system, the Citizens Amendment also facilitates systems thinking. It would help us to raise our consciousness about how things really work so we can address issues with more awareness and greater intelligence.

A personal story helps illustrate this. A few years back, I took a walk down the hill from my house, through some woods to meet a new neighbor. When I arrived, he was digging a series of trenches to handle the runoff from a recent rain. I stopped to talk with him for awhile and marveled at all he had done. Then, walking back up the hill, rather than following the path, I followed the course of the water. A few weeks earlier, I had been doing some work on our gravel driveway. A small chasm had formed across it, so I had smoothed it out and redirected the water to flow down a gully nearby. Unknowingly, I had shifted the runoff from the top of the hill and sent

159

it down to my neighbor's house. Embarrassed to realize this, I quickly and easily solved his problem with a few strokes of the shovel. In fact, I solved his problem more completely than anything he could do on his property.

This story illustrates several points: 1) It's valuable to see and understand the system before correcting a symptom. I might have noticed where I was sending the runoff before fixing my driveway, and my neighbor would have done better to walk upstream to see where the water was coming from before building his trench network. 2) When things are connected into a system, it is often possible to discover a little change that can have an immense effect. My few turns with the shovel outweighed his days of work. 3) With a living system, it's not just finding points of leverage that can matter, but being in relationship. That is, for my insight to help him, I needed to be willing to make the slight sacrifice of effort on my end so he could gain a great deal.

Our current political system works pretty much the opposite. Rather than helping us understand the big picture and encouraging us to sacrifice a little for the benefit of all, it promotes an atomistic viewpoint, where we see only our own point of view, and are encouraged to act from self-interest.

When legislators act in the general interest, they are often penalized because systems thinking among voters is lacking. In my state of Washington, there was a citizens' initiative to repeal a high motor vehicle registration tax. Since there is no income tax in this state, it was one of few progressive taxes where the rich are taxed more than the poor. It sought to penalize the use of cars and transfer funds to the development of mass transit. But, of course, car dealers felt victimized. With a vested interest in automobile sales and usage, they came together to work for the repeal of the tax.

The choice was presented to voters in an emotional way: how unfair it was for the people of this state to pay more for licenses than those in other states. There was no one to present the systems perspective. The general interest viewpoint could hardly be heard, so the special interests were again successful.

Government, which supposedly represents the public interest, is forbidden to express an opinion in these matters. In fact, its role to act in the public interest is under siege by special interests. They insist that government be run like a business and view citizens as customers. They are lobbying to privatize government functions—like prisons, electric utilities, welfare, or education—as though the public good will be served by market competition. As the voices of the public good are diminished, there is less and less involvement and consciousness from citizens about what is happening. Implementing a Wisdom Council changes this. It sets up a way for everyone to see deeply into what's going on and to start grappling with the systemic nature of issues.

Layers of a System

This is not to say that the Citizens Amendment is the only approach that is systemic; there are others. But the Citizens Amendment acts at the deepest layer of the system. Without it, the other efforts will not be as effective as they might. Here's a group exercise that illustrates this point.

There were about fifty people divided into teams, and each team was to build a tower from a collection of differently shaped blocks. The teams had to work in silence, taking turns, adding one block at a time until all were used.

Once the exercise began, I noticed that a few teams were proceeding faster than my team. They had positioned their initial blocks differently and it allowed them much greater stability. I could see that, unless we made a similar adjustment to our base, we were going to waste time struggling to balance each added block, and eventually fail in the overall task.

The rules prohibited talking, so I tried signaling. But my teammates were busy attending to the difficulties of adding each new block. So when my next turn came, I pulled down our tower.

My team was temporarily stunned, but I used my turn to reposition the foundation block. Now, starting again, it was easy to add blocks and we progressed rapidly. After the exercise was over we talked. Now all could see that this action was necessary. Without it we would've worked longer and harder at each successive layer of the tower, but our ultimate success was dependent on the position of the foundation block. By attending to that layer first, we made the efforts at all different layers pay off.

The Citizens Amendment is a similar adjustment to the foundation block of society's tower, making everyone's work more effective. But we need not tear down society's tower to make the needed adjustment. In fact, the Citizens Amendment doesn't actually change the foundation block, the constitutional process. It uses it to facilitate change at yet a deeper layer, in We the People. Adding the Citizens Amendment is like standing on the bottom layer of society's tower and planting a seed in the soil at its foot. From this seed grows wisdom and understanding in all of us, like a vine extending up and around the tower. The vine changes the nature of the overall system from mechanical to organic, and builds both stability and flexibility.

The U.S. Constitution is the focus of a number of efforts to "change the system." Term limits for elected officials, or an amendment to revoke corporate "personhood," or instituting a system of proportional representation are examples. These seek changes to the first layer of the tower. The Citizens Amendment aims deeper, to We the People and the quality of our thinking, way down to Layer 0.

Layer 0: We the People

When people first hear about the Amendment, one of the most frequent questions they ask is, "Why does it need to be an amendment? Why not just do it?" The tower metaphor provides a way to answer. Just doing it would provide marvelous improvements to society's tower in the upper layers. It might generate more feeling of involvement in citizens or more understanding. It could help to improve legislation. It could build community. But it wouldn't create a legitimately mandated voice of We the People. Only the U.S. Constitution can do that. Only through it, do We the People act and reassume control over the system.

After Dr. Deming's Red Bead Experiment was over, he would often ask his willing workers how they felt during the exercise. Although each knew that the results were entirely random, and even though they may have been laughing at the time, virtually all of them reported that they felt responsible for their performance. They "tried," whatever that means here, to manufacture white beads instead of red, and they felt badly when the results were poor.

In the same way, we *try* to do better in our current system, but we always seem to have a certain percentage of people dealing in drugs or being poor or the same small number of creative geniuses. In our Game system, most people at the bottom of the scale work hard to improve economically. We should celebrate their progress as individuals. But in the aggregate, the whole bottom half of the income curve hasn't gained in more than 20 years, while the very richest bound farther ahead. We talk about those in poverty as though they just aren't working hard enough, and about the rich as though they earned every penny, but both are really just products of the system.

In the same way, we talk as though we care deeply about the well being of the planet, our real wealth. Surely we all feel that the continued survival of human civilization on this planet is important. But to not pay attention to our system, when it is in charge, belies that we care. The system directs our attention to other things—like "getting ahead," economic growth, and shallow chatter about celebrities and various entertainments.

Empowerment

Yes, the system has power over us. But this book is *not* saying that we are victims of its power. It's saying the opposite, that if we become conscious of the system and how it works, then we have power over it. We are only powerless as long as we deny the existence of the system and its impact on us, and remain ignorant of our ability to change it.

True empowerment is not just proclaiming and believing that "we create our reality," as though all can be done through meditation and inner work. Those are important; they may even be preconditions. But true empowerment arises from Choice-creating, from facing the really important issues creatively, from experiencing breakthrough insights and shifts of awareness, and from taking thoughtful actions jointly.

— 11 —

Creating Shared Vision (Level 3)

. . . there are people, many people in the world who look to America as its great hope. And do we have some answer for these people other than 'believe in a market economy'? I mean if people overthrow the great narrative of Lenin and Marx as they've done in many places and we applaud them. And they turn to us and say 'do you have some narrative that we may be able to adopt and adapt? . . . Where will we get new narratives that will give people a sense of dignity and hope? People look to America. Do we have an answer for them?

Neil Postman, in an interview with Scott London on *Insight and Outlook*

*V*ision is the third model of how change happens. From this model arises a viewpoint and level of thinking that offers a different way of gauging the impact of the Citizens Amendment. In using this word "vision," we mean something larger than just a picture of the future or what our ego desires. A vision makes us a part of something meaningful that perhaps this familiar story will illustrate: During the Middle Ages, a traveler came across a group of men working on a large project. The traveler asked one what he was doing and he said, "I am laying bricks." Farther along, he asked a second man who said, "I am earning a living for my family." Later still, he asked a third man who answered, "I am building a cathedral."

This last man had a vision. And because of it, his motivation was richer than dutifully doing his job or purposefully serving his family. A vision has more power for us than even the urge to survive. Throughout history, for instance, many Americans have willingly sacrificed their lives for our shared vision of democracy, equality and justice for all.

Furthermore, a vision can inspire people to do more and be more than they, or anyone else, thought was possible. It draws people out and coordinates them and their actions to become part of something larger than themselves.

The Human Need for Vision

In his book, *Surely, You're Joking, Dr. Feynman,* Nobel prize-winning physicist, Dr. Richard Feynman, tells the story of how, during World War II, he helped his employees shift from "just doing their jobs" to "sharing a vision." He was manager of the computing unit at Los Alamos National Laboratory, where the nation's top physicists were assembled in a secret effort to build an atomic bomb. Soldiers and civilians used calculating machines to "run the numbers" on complex math problems. They had little idea of the meaning of their work and watched as the war seemingly progressed without them.

When Dr. Feynman was asked to take over the unit, he said he would do so only if he could explain to the workers what they were doing. Because of the need for secrecy, his superiors balked. But in the end, they granted him the opportunity to speak freely—for 15 minutes only.

During that brief time, Dr. Feynman explained to all the workers exactly what their calculations meant and how they related to the war effort. It was like flipping a switch to turn on the organization. Beforehand, the workers were merely running numbers. Afterwards, they held a shared vision of how they were winning the war! Almost immediately, productivity went up nine-fold.

In society, Martin Luther King did the same thing for many Americans when he stood on the steps of the Lincoln Memorial and articulated a vision that brought people together and called forth excellence from them. He said:

> *I have a dream . . . that one day this nation will rise up and live out the true meaning of its creed: 'We hold these truths to be self-evident that all men are created equal.'*
>
> *I have a dream . . . that one day on the red hills of Georgia the sons of former slaves and the sons of former slave owners will be able to sit down together at a table of brotherhood.*
>
> *I have a dream . . . that my four children will one day live in a nation where they will not be judged by the color of their skin but by the content of their character.*

These words established a vision in the minds and hearts of many that continues to inspire people throughout the world.

The Citizens Amendment would build shared vision among all citizens in two ways: 1) It would reconnect us to, and help fulfill, the already established vision of democracy laid down at the founding; and 2) It would provide an ongoing process of creating new vision for the future.

Our Vision of Democracy

Unlike most countries, which were founded on ethnicity or territory, the United States was founded on a vision. We coalesced around a set of ideas, "that all men are created equal, that they are endowed by their Creator with certain inalienable rights, that among these are life, liberty and the pursuit of happiness." We hold that government derives its "just powers from the consent of the governed."

These were radical ideas that painted an inspiring vision to people in the eighteenth century. Everyone then felt part of a delicate experiment. But citizens today are less inspired by this vision. In a *National Civic Review* article, John Gardner wonders about this and asks, "How can the American people be awakened to a new sense of purpose, a new vision and a new resolve?" (*National Civic Review,* Fall-Winter '94)

Interestingly, the Founders held a different vision for democracy than we do today. When they referred to "the people," they were really only referring to an elite subset—white male property holders. And they did not trust this group to self-govern. They were looking to an elite of the elite to serve as elected officials. And even then, they did not just let them make decisions, but established a balance of powers and a voting process to put the system in control. The legislative model they liked was the Parliament of Great Britain, with a House of Lords for the aristocrats and a lower House for the commoners. They assumed that two classes of people would always be present, so they split the legislative function into two chambers to account for it, the Senate and the House of Representatives. In the original design, they only let "the people" elect members of the "lower" House. The president and senators were chosen by legislators.

The Founders wanted a republic, not a democracy, and they created one that worked. This was a great accomplishment! Beyond that, they also had a second great innovation. They created a vision of true democracy in the minds and hearts of people all over the world. First, in their wording of the Declaration of Independence they said, "We hold these truths to be self-evident, that all men are created equal . . ." At the time, it was almost universally believed that all people were *not* created equal. Then, eleven years later, they phrased the Preamble to the U.S. Constitution to say, *"We the People of the United States, in Order to form a more perfect Union, establish Justice, insure domestic Tranquility, provide for the common defense, promote the general Welfare, and secure the Blessings of Liberty to ourselves and our Posterity, do ordain and establish this Constitution for the United States of America."*

The phrase "We the People . . . do ordain and establish . . ." planted the notion that all of us can come together on occasion to consider our situation and reach wise consensus on what to do. This phrasing implies that true democracy is possible and, indeed, that we achieved it to found the United States.

But this isn't what really happened, nor is it what they meant to say. As the Constitutional Convention wound down, a rough draft was handed to a small committee for refinement. It began "We the people of the States of New Hampshire, Massachusetts Bay, etc. . . ." going on to list all thirteen states, even though only twelve had sent delegates.

Gouverneur Morris, a gifted writer, was asked to edit the document. Like most others, Mr. Morris was fearful of democracy, stating earlier at the convention, "There never was, nor ever will be a civilized society without an aristocracy." In fact, he made a suggestion during the deliberations, that to realize the benefits of an aristocracy, the members of the Senate should be appointed for life by the president.

In the editing of the newly drafted document, however, Gouverneur Morris was faced with a dilemma. The convention had already decided that the Constitution would go into effect after nine of the thirteen states approved. Since no one could be sure which states would approve, the document couldn't start with a list of the states. To resolve the problem and shorten the phrase, Gouverneur Morris changed the acting agent in the sentence to, "We the People of the United States . . . " This editing decision must have seemed minor at the time. It was convenient and almost said what the delegates wanted to say.

But to say "We the People of the United States . . . do ordain . . ." is to invite a new and powerful actor into being and onto the world stage, and to invoke a new vision of how societies can structure and govern themselves. It was a vision of true democracy that people eventually came to believe had already happened. Three quarters of a century later, Abraham Lincoln picked up on this theme and took it a step further in his Gettysburg address, describing the founding as though it was "of the people, by the people, for the people," even though that really wasn't what happened. So it is natural for many people today to think we were handed a democracy by the Founders, but have been squandering it ever since. Clearly, that is not the case.

We also talk as though other countries are democracies because they have elections. But that is not true either. The vision of true democracy has yet to be realized. The Citizens Amendment would make it more achievable.

Creating a New Vision

A vision is about marshalling and directing human energy. Martin Luther King was able to create a shared vision, for example, because his words were uttered in a time of crisis, when the injustices of racial segregation had fired a seething anger. This was also true for the vision that John F. Kennedy set when he proposed putting a man on the moon by the end of the 1960's. He spoke right after the launching of Sputnik, when people were afraid of losing the "race to space" to the Communists. Abraham Lincoln, Mahatma Gandhi, Tom Paine, and Nelson Mandela all had platforms of crisis from which to launch their visions. Through words and deeds, all were able to redirect the energy of fear, anger and resentment toward something new and vital.

The Citizens Amendment also creates vision from energy. With it, We the People select and confront urgent, seemingly impossible-to-solve issues, and address them through Choice-creating. In the midst of facing these real crises, we articulate statements of vision.

For example, some employees and managers in a steam plant at a paper mill met in a series of four Choice-creating meetings. First, they listed a number of possible issues to address, like the need for better cleanup, more training, and the distrust between operators and the maintenance department. In categorizing and sorting through these issues, it became clear that there was one issue more central than the others. It was the ash that hung in the air of the plant.

Everyone knew that the mill was running at twice its design capacity, and that ash was an inevitable result. Engineers had been trying to fix the problem for years and believed that only a major investment would solve it. The employee union and management had already tangled on this issue, but since it gave the mill its competitive advantage, everyone had backed away.

In the first meeting, the group chose this crucial issue to work on, but did so hesitantly because it seemed impossible to solve. They wrote this problem statement on the board: "How to get rid of the caustic black ash?" By agreeing on the importance of this issue, and by stating it as the challenge, it became a shared vision that motivated people throughout the mill.

Employees talked about it all the time, on the job, on their breaks, and even at home. Maintenance people started experimenting with solutions, listening to ideas that the operators had been telling them for years. Operators started listening to maintenance people, too, and adjusted their procedures in important ways. Great progress was made until two people who hadn't been to any meetings got caught up in the excitement and invented a new and patentable device, which solved 90% of the remaining problem.

The Power of Visioning

The key to solving the mill's "impossible" problem was little more than clarifying it and acknowledging that it needed solving. Just doing this sparked a new spirit of cooperation and creativity that actually did solve the problem. It changed working relationships and thinking styles in people. As Steven Covey, A. Roger Merrill, and Rebecca R. Merrill say in their book, *First Things First*, "The power of transcendent vision is greater than the power of the scripting deep inside the human personality and it subordinates it, submerges it, until the whole personality is reorganized in the accomplishment of that vision. The passion of *shared* vision empowers people to transcend the petty, negative interactions that consume so much time and effort and deplete the quality of life."

The visioning process by itself can often make an essential difference. In science today, there is strong evidence that just getting clear on what we want and expressing it can help manifest it. As quantum physicist, Fred Alan Wolfe, said in his book, *Mind into Matter: A New Alchemy of Science and Spirit*, "Quantum physics and modern computers add a new view of how our words—the stuff of our minds—alter and shape the world we all take for granted as 'out there.' In effect, there is no 'out there' out there unless there is first and primarily an 'in here' taking action—one having a deep transformative effect—on the world 'out there.'"

In their book, *Breakpoint and Beyond,* George Land and Beth Jarman emphasize the power of visioning by focusing on the difference between what they call "future-pull" versus "cause-push". Cause-push is the normal way we think about change, as though life is pushed into the future by events in the past. Future-pull is the Level 3 way of thinking about change, which is more consistent with the nature of living beings. Acorns, for instance, are better understood as future oak trees than as the end result of the forces acting on seeds. The authors say, "New discoveries in biology and psychology join with those that caused so much consternation in physics. They underscore how we—and every other part of nature—are being pulled to the future."

Visionary Leadership

Like the mill workers who identified the key problem in their workplace and established a vision of what they wanted, the Citizens Wisdom Council will also identify key challenges in society and describe what we want. No matter what issue they identify—"How do we become sustainable as a culture?" or "How might we better educate our children?" or "How might we become a wise democracy?"—it will generate the benefits of shared vision, orienting people to be more curious, to be open-minded and creative, and to act for positive change.

Consider, for example, if the Wisdom Council started with a list of problems with government, like people's distrust of government, the inordinate corporate influence over legislation, limited bipartisan cooperation, or how citizens seem apathetic and don't vote. Let's say the Wisdom Council decided that a point of leverage in addressing these issues is to reform the way political campaigns are financed, but they couldn't get any more specific.

No problem. Just putting it out there focuses attention on this issue and on the available options for campaign finance reform, and enlists creative thinking to develop more options. This vision of what is needed will spark new behaviors by office holders, corporations, citizens, and contributors to campaigns. It will build a constituency for reform that is ready to support new ideas.

By creating shared vision in this way, the Citizens Amendment structures a new style of leadership into society. Currently, we wait until problems impose themselves on us before we take action, usually through some coercive act by Congress. But with a new capacity for building shared vision, we become pro-active rather than reactive. South African consultant Oz Swallow described this new approach as facing forward instead of backward. He said we have a choice. We can either go through life identifying what we don't want and striving to avoid that, or we can identify what we do want and aim for that.

Let me illustrate the difference between these two styles. Once I consulted in two different manufacturing plants, Chip's and Dale's. The people who worked in Chip's plant were just supposed to work and not complain. When problems arose, Chip brought in experts who would suggest new procedures or new devices. Often, the employees would resist these changes.

In Dale's plant, the employees held regular Choice-creating meetings to work on important issues. They set targets in different areas, like production, quality, or trust. It was a high-performing environment, with machines continually being improved by the people who operated them. And over time, the employees became experts.

Chip had more crises in his mill than Dale did. Key machines would break down more frequently, quality control problems would arise, employees would get in fights, there were more union grievances, and customers would be upset. When a crisis occurred, experts would meet and the employees would see them strutting about importantly, relishing their VIP status. In Dale's plant, production was better, quality was better, and problems that might become crises didn't gain an easy foothold. When a problem did arise, people would come together and solve it.

Of course, the management style of our society is currently Chip's, not Dale's. We wait for problems to arise before we start work on them. Citizens are like workers in the plant, mostly uninvolved with the issues of the day, waiting for the experts to make their pronouncements, and then complaining about them when they do. But the Citizens Amendment changes us to Dale's style. It invites our participation in regular meetings so that we understand issues and start running the place. With it, we build a vision of what we are trying to achieve and help one another in getting there.

It is healthier too. When people have a vision, they feel more in control of their lives and jobs, and have fewer health problems, particularly heart problems. In his book, *Man's Search for Meaning*, Victor Frankl described how vision can even be essential to survival. In his concentration camp experience during World War II, he noticed that the key determining factor for the survival of his fellow inmates was whether or not they held a positive vision for when they got out. These positive phenomena are not well understood, but they are real. They portend some of the magical benefits of enacting the Citizens Amendment and switching to a visionary style of leadership.

Institutional Change

This change to a visionary leadership style would have positive effects on the workings of key institutions in society, like the media and government.

We frequently complain about the negativity of the media, how it puts sensationalism, conflicts, crimes, accidents, and scandals constantly in the headlines. But this is only natural when we are facing backwards as a society, focusing on what we don't want, rather than what we do want.

But with a shared vision for society, our interest is just as naturally aroused at positive news. It's a different organizing principle. Take World War II, for example, when we shared a vision of winning the war. Any positive progress on the battle front was what people were interested in. Crimes and such, to the extent they even occurred, went to the back pages of the papers.

The way to fix today's negative media isn't so much to encourage self-censorship in the media, as it is to build a shared vision in society. Then, even if the media still engages in a head-long rush for ratings and profits, we will be taken forward instead of backward.

Consider the effects of visionary leadership on government. Currently, our civil servants have the worst possible top executive, John Q. Public. He is judgmental, critical, reactive, and blame-seeking. He has no idea of what he wants, just what he doesn't want. Government executives and elected leaders can't talk with John Q, nor do they have any trust that he won't change his mind from moment to moment. And since they are likely to get pilloried for any entrepreneurial step, they naturally protect themselves by becoming bureaucratic and doing things by the book.

Also, John Q. Public doesn't trust his employees, the civil servants, and tries to control their actions in ways that make them even more bureaucratic. Rather than building a system of trust so that the public servant can be effective, he seeks to hedge them in with regulations, to measure every output and commoditize their work. He doesn't trust that people want to serve others and assumes only that they will serve themselves. Through his distrust, he unknowingly promotes this attitude.

But with the Citizens Amendment, John Q. Public would be transformed into We the People—a visionary, facilitative, compassionate leader. We would articulate a clear vision of what we all want and support government employees as they help us to achieve it.

Like it or not, the natural inclination of people toward promoting their own self-interest over the general interest cannot be the basis for our future together. This orientation will not serve us as well as it has in the past. We must help reorient people to serve the public interest. This is not so hard a change as it might seem. It merely requires a meaningful shared vision of what we all want. This aims both us and government toward the same ends and changes our civil servants into "us" instead of "them."

With the Citizens Amendment in place, we merely figure out what the key issues are and then figure out what we want. That's the hard work. The solutions are free to manifest themselves.

Part IV

TRANSFORMING SOCIETY

(LEVEL 4)

Die and Become. 'Til thou has learnt this, thou art but a dull guest on this dark planet.

Johann Göethe

— 12 —

"Turning On" Our System

Your qualities cannot be discovered until you are tested by a crisis. . . . If it is your intention to surmount a crisis and if you are willing to be at risk and go beyond what you know you can, then qualities that were unsuspected will emerge. . . . So, if you find yourself in an awful mess, that allows you to become great. . . . Indeed this is the only process by which greatness comes about.

Oz Swallow, South African Consultant

*T*here is an old joke about a guy who goes to the store to buy a chainsaw. The clerk shows him a gas model and promises that with it, he can cut at least four cords of wood a day. When the man gets home, he works as hard as he can, but cuts only one. Dissatisfied, he takes the chainsaw back to the store and complains. The clerk looks the equipment over. It seems fine. He adjusts the choke, pulls the cord, and starts the motor. With that, the man jumps up, and exclaims, "What's that noise?"

(pregnant pause)

We the People are like this, too. We don't seem to know that our system, with us in it, can be turned on. Instead, we just work harder at the situation we've been handed. But when we do this, the important problems we face go unattended, and our true potential remains untapped until one of the issues we face reaches crisis proportions. Sometimes then, in those special circumstances, we do "turn on." We pull together, get creative, and overcome the crisis. This is what happened in World War II, for instance. But we mostly avoid dealing with the big issues, and stay turned off instead, implementing stopgap measures.

Crises are a time of wrenching trauma. But they also offer the possibility of releasing vast hidden potential. It is in such times that the greatness of people like Martin Luther King, Jr., Abraham Lincoln, George Washington, and Franklin D. Roosevelt is discovered.

Franklin D. Roosevelt, for instance, was a lightweight politician, a glad-hander, and a mama's boy, until he suffered a polio attack. Rising to meet this personal challenge, he grew in depth, inner strength, and in sympathy for others. His personal crisis could have driven him to solitude and bitterness. Instead, it helped him realize the capabilities that were within him.

Crisis as a Creative Tool

For eons, people have created artificial crises to spark their capabilities. Hard-nosed managers in organizations, for example, will often set a goal that seems outrageous. If people accept the challenge, it creates a kind of crisis for them and they will come together and sometimes pull off a miracle. Good artists do it as well, making the creative experience a personal crisis.

Games are another way to tap this potential. Because there is only one winner, each team faces an artificial crisis. We've probably all seen football games where, with just a few minutes left, one team will find themselves behind, catch fire, and snatch victory from the jaws of defeat. At the last moment, there is a rush of energy and new capability that turns the game around—an energy burst that involves those watching, as well. This is part of the fun of being a spectator and rooting for the underdog. If you vicariously identify with such a team, you can participate in this "turned on" experience when it happens.

Another example is when students wait until the night before an assignment is due to start working on it. From a logical perspective, it makes no sense to waste so much time beforehand, but by waiting they create enough of a crisis to spark the release of their creative flow.

For a crisis to "turn on" latent energy, it requires a sense of urgency. Consider the example of the crayfish. If the claw of a crayfish is held firm and food is placed just out of reach, the crayfish will starve to death. But if it's trapped in the same way and a predator comes along, the crayfish will jettison its claw and scramble to safety. Only in this case is the urgency of the crisis strong enough for the crayfish to drop old patterns, respond anew, and turn on. I've seen this happen in a work environment, as well.

One time, I was an inexperienced new employee of a timber company, suggesting an idea to the manager of a plywood mill. It was the last redwood plywood mill in operation. I proposed using fir or hemlock, cheaper grades of wood for the inner portions of the plywood. This would save valuable redwood for the outer face. Hearing this, the manager smiled at me and patiently explained why it wouldn't work; there were different expansion properties of these woods and the glue couldn't hold them together.

About two years later, the mill was in grave financial straits. I was attending another meeting and heard his boss ask him if there would be any problem using fir for the inner portions of the plywood. "No problem," he said, "We can do that."

The second time, his boss was speaking and the situation was dire. It forced this manager to open his mind to new possibilities and develop new options. In the end it worked, but by then it was too late. The mill closed shortly thereafter.

The Wisdom Council helps us use the power of crises by identifying an issue and highlighting its urgency. With We the People participating vicariously, it's an opportunity for all of society to turn on, as well.

In the first chapter of this book, you were asked, "What is fundamentally the most significant problem we face as a society?" This is an unusual question because it invites people to think outside of the box—to focus on seemingly impossible-to-solve issues. Normally, we steer away from them like the mill manager did.

In fact, if you were in a meeting with a group of well-meaning citizens and legislators trying to improve things, and you suggested that the group address one of these impossible issues, they would probably look at you funny. They might try to get you to be "realistic," or to change your mind; you might hear words like, "Let's not waste time on something we can't solve. Let's work on what we can do something about." You might be encouraged to stay within what is popularly referred to as your "circle of influence." A politician at the meeting might remind everyone that, even if the group were to devise a creative answer, he would never get reelected if he seriously proposed it.

The Wisdom Council frees us from these thinking "boxes" that come as part of our current system. Instead, it helps us recognize that people can break out of the box, turn on, and magically solve the impossible. It is designed to elicit a creative response from all of us.

Turning on an Organization

In the early 1980's, I watched a large sawmill become turned-on using a process very much like the Wisdom Council. As with most manufacturing plants at that time, it contained two types of employees, hourly and salaried. Salaried employees were part of the company, mostly supervisors. They were paid whether the mill was operating or not. On the other hand, hourly employees were paid by the hour. They were considered a cost of production, part of the machinery of the mill. They were supposed to just do their job and not complain. But this arrangement was breaking down. Because of government regulations and adversarial union relations, supervisors were limited in how much they could discipline employees. One supervisor told me that he felt like a "one-legged man in an ass-kicking contest." He complained that when it came to disciplining employees, the company no longer backed him up.

It was during this time that I proposed an experiment to management, something from Japan called "Quality Circles." With Quality Circles, hourly employees are trained, supported by management, and gathered for one hour each week to solve problems in the mill. It promised higher productivity, better quality, and happier employees. Management only liked part of the idea—the part that would result in less trouble from employees. They did not want to be involved themselves, nor did they approve any training. They just wanted employees to feel better about their jobs so problems with discipline would decline.

In theory, this was a prescription for disaster. Without management involvement or employee training, our program was doomed. But in fact, it worked much better than other programs. It transformed the employees, management, and the productivity of the mill. Two employee teams were formed, one for each shift. There were no supervisors interested in attending, so I facilitated them like Wisdom Councils, where the rest of the mill was aware and interested, curious to see what would happen.

I started the first meeting by asking, "What are some of the issues we might work on?" and we made a list. In the beginning, it was difficult for the employees to think this freely. They had been taught over the years to only do what they were told. On the few previous occasions where they went to meetings, management would talk at them and they were supposed to listen. But here it was different. Employees were not being told anything, not even what to work on. They were being asked what they cared about and chose what that was.

Both employee groups began by expressing their frustration with the foremen, the company, with one another, and even with the union. Some wanted revenge, to get the foreman fired, or to get some kind of special treatment. Most felt themselves to be victims and were generally angry about their circumstances.

A normal Quality Circle program would purposefully avoid these emotional topics. Those programs train employees to only address what is in their work areas and teach them to follow a rational, step-by-step problem-solving procedure. But in Wisdom Council fashion, the workers here were facilitated to address what was important to them and to use Choice-creating.

At first, the group got into negative-toned, "impossible" issues, like getting the foreman fired. But as the dialogue unfolded, the issue changed. Someone would say, for example, "You know, the foreman isn't really that bad if you get to know him outside of work." Then, they would talk about that and grow in their understanding of what the pressures on him must be like. Anger would subside and a new problem statement would come up that had more interest for them, like "management doesn't respect people." In the end, both groups decided that the real problem was a lack of trust between management and employees. So they started working on this.

Just by choosing this issue, they started relating better to the supervisor and to management. They made improvements to the equipment and to the methods. They began asking the supervisors for help on projects and this made the supervisors feel good.

Others in the mill could see these changed attitudes and it rubbed off, and they participated as well. Before long, without realizing it, the two groups had addressed and solved the most important issue they faced: the lack of trust in the mill. They shifted their way of thinking to Choice-creating and "turned on." And the rest of the employees and management were going along with them.

Interestingly, it was hard for them to appreciate the extent of the changes they were making. The environment became different, but they had also become different, so the changes didn't seem so great to them. At one point, someone complained, "We haven't made any progress in these meetings." The charts from the first meeting were presented to them. There was silence because people almost didn't recognize their own words. Finally, someone said, "That is ancient history." The group didn't want to go back there.

Turning on the People

The Citizens Amendment promises changes to society like those that happened at the mill. It promises that average groups of people can similarly come together, be caring and creative, and solve problems, bringing all of us along with them.

Before the meetings, hourly employees were just putting in time. They saw problems and cared, but the structure of the situation provided no way to become involved. But the meetings started people talking. Through them the real and pressing issues were addressed and the door was opened for all to become more themselves and to participate. No one wanted to be wasteful or inefficient, everyone wanted a safe environment, they liked providing quality service to others, and they felt pride in their products.

Here is one employee's "turned on" moment. For many years, the senior employee on day shift had seemed too old to run the most important piece of equipment in the mill. All logs that came into the mill funneled through his machine, but he ran it inefficiently. Because of his seniority and union rules, it was his right to stay in that position and, as a result, production for the whole shift was curtailed.

Management used to joke that it would be worthwhile to pay him not to work and put him up in a condominium in the Bahamas, just so someone else could run the machine.

This man had always considered himself a good employee because he did what he was told. But one day, during a meeting of his group, they were looking at a chart of mill production. He suddenly stood up and exclaimed, "That's not right!" In that instant, even though he had seen this chart many times, he realized that it was his machine that caused the production gap between the shifts. From that moment on, the production gap disappeared. It was a transformation inside one man's mind where, because of the atmosphere in the meeting, he caught fire. It had dramatic results for the mill.

These Wisdom Council type meetings flipped a similar invisible switch in the minds of most everyone in the mill. Workers started recognizing how much they cared, and many started taking more responsibility. They became experts on their machines and supervised repairs. They made friends with one another and with management.

Twenty months after the mill workers began their meetings, Sacramento Bee correspondent, Bill Israel, interviewed some of them for an article, "At this Sawmill, All the 'Bickering's Just Gone Away,' " (Sept. 12, 1983). He called what he discovered, "industrial magic," with increased production, new feelings of trust, and people just feeling better. He wrote, "Some men are reporting improvements in their physical health that they attribute to the change in the mill's working atmosphere since the program began."

But because this change was happening bottom-up and not top-down, it was sometimes difficult for top managers in the company to adjust. One day, a vice president from headquarters was taking a tour through the mill and saw some of these new behaviors. Even though mill performance was exceptional, it upset him that people had so much freedom. He saw one employee adjust his own machine and told him to leave the controls to his foreman. Then he rebuked the foreman for shirking his duties. Then he was upset at the superintendent for his "lax" style.

The mill's new self-management, which produced far better results than top-down control, felt threatening to this manager. His outburst deeply hurt the employee to whom he first spoke. This person wanted to resume his old attitude. He told himself, "Why should I care? I get paid the same either way. I'll just go back to my old ways, take no responsibility, and do what I'm told." But it wasn't so easy to stuff those feelings anymore, because now he knew he cared.

He returned to the meetings where everyone could discuss the incident. They realized how threatening these changes must seem to some managers. Later, they invited the vice president to come to one of their meetings and, later yet, to attend one of their presentations. The hourly employees began exercising leadership on the whole system.

The spreading change was a redefinition of Real Life. At first, the meetings were just a break from the normal workday. That is, Real Life was normal work, and the meetings were an interlude. But over time, things switched around. The authentic conversation in the meetings became Real Life and work seemed like the interlude. This openness and authenticity extended beyond the meetings to the whole organization.

However, once in a while, the meetings would stop because things got too busy or because of scheduling problems. If this went on too long, the system would begin to revert back to the old ways. The most important function of the meetings, even more important than the decisions and innovations that resulted, was the different dynamic that they sparked in the mill. It was their ability to "turn on" the mill to the Circle mentality that was making the big difference. When that happened, productivity soared, quality went up, management-union relations improved, everyone became happier, people grew in capabilities, and the employees brought many of these changes home with them. Often I heard people say that what they learned from the meetings affected how they talked to their spouses and their children.

This transformation was *not* achieved by asking people to try harder. No one was being asked to do something they didn't want to do. The changes came via the process, facing crises with others in a way that encouraged all to be creative. And even though most people were not part of the meetings at first, the issues and concerns that were raised interested everyone. At the end of the first year of meetings, all the foremen met to determine whether they would officially support the meeting process and become involved or not. Before they decided, I asked one supervisor how he felt about it. He waited before he answered and then tears formed in his eyes. He said, "I didn't know these people could be like this." He felt remorse about how he had treated them before. He had changed and they had changed. All foremen decided to support the process and get involved.

Once the employees started thinking creatively, every machine and every function in the mill started improving. One group of employees identified the most important problem they faced as the need for "more clean up." Because this function was inadequate, loose bark was getting into the equipment, causing safety and production problems. They tackled the worst hang up first, where huge logs had to be unnecessarily jostled around, then completely eliminated that problem with a 20-minute welding job. It was a simple, permanent change that was far better than adding more clean-up people.

In another case, a group of twelve maintenance workers were unanimously adamant about needing an additional full-time person to oil machinery. Again, once they started Choice-creating, they developed a plan that more than solved the problem without the additional person. Part of the solution was that they invented a new oiling device that saved about 20 hours a week—which is like hiring a person half-time. They also changed lubricant types, made new job classifications, and established a new training program, which the state eventually funded.

When the employee meetings started, no one in management imagined the extent of the impact on the mill and the people. The intent of it was for hourly employees to cause less trouble. Instead, workers took on management responsibility and sparked substantial productivity and quality increases, as well as changes in their personal lives.

The Citizens Amendment Would Turn On Society

The Citizens Amendment sets up something very similar for society, placing a group of ordinary citizens on center stage. It structures a way for all of us, through them, to face the crisis issues together and to turn on.

How unusual this is only became clear to me in my Dynamic Facilitation seminars. People would break into small Choice-creating groups and choose societal issues on which to work. At first, they were anxious about their ability to make any real headway. But after a while, they would begin Choice-creating. At this point, I would interrupt and ask them to notice that, even though they may still feel some confusion, they were doing something exceptional. They were thinking at a very high level while addressing the most important societal issues. People were listening to one another, they were interested in different ideas, and everyone was seeking what is best for all, not just for themselves. "Where else in society is this happening?" I would ask. "In Congress? In think tanks? In university research labs? In corporations? In non-profit organizations?"

Unfortunately, the answer to this question may be "nowhere." Because of the structure of our system, the really important issues do not get the attention they deserve. And if they do get it, the process is not Choice-creating. It's a battle among special interests about some specific, marginal proposal.

Once people establish the Choice-creating dynamic, they escape from the Box that contains them. They feel empowered and realize that, with creativity, they can solve any problem. This is what happened in the mill, and what can happen with us in our burgeoning democracy. As currently structured, we teach and encourage people to not care about the big issues, that we really can't affect them anyway, that we should just attend to our own lives and jobs, and to be critical of the decisions that "management" hands down.

A former neighbor of mine illustrates this attitude. For years, I listened to him complain about his job in government. He would either be frustrated and tense about his work, or say he didn't really care, telling me he was just putting in his time until retirement. Then, he retired and was about to move. He had, in his words, "beat the system." During one of our last conversations, he started to rail against politicians. He complained that they were only out for themselves and had little interest in really helping society. I pointed out that this was the same attitude he had when he was working. He acknowledged this truth and said, "Well, what can you do?"

I believe all politicians care deeply about the general welfare, just as all mill workers really care about the quality of their work. But our system redirects this caring to the Game. A few years ago, when I was attending a college reunion, I overheard two old classmates describing their entrepreneurial good fortune. They had purchased wind-powered electrical generators and were making a huge return on their investment. As they continued talking, the focus of their enthusiasm struck me as odd. Rather than taking pride in the contribution they were making to society—helping the world transition to renewable energy—their pride was in their personal rewards, how they were winning the Game. This is what our system encourages.

To release our deep potential and to attain excellence, we must face the real crises of our situation. The Citizens Amendment helps us do this. It helps us to turn on—both as individuals and as a society.

— 13 —

Choosing to BE

It is our self-reflective consciousness that gives us the capacity to recognize the inevitable consequences of continuing on our present path. It is, therefore, the key to our salvation.

David Korten, *Post-Corporate World*

*T*ransformation is a magical process, the most common illustration of which is a caterpillar becoming a butterfly. The caterpillar does not manage this process. It just stops eating and builds a cocoon, trusting the natural forces of life.

It is a change process that also operates in us, only sometimes we get in its way by trying to control things. For many aspects of life, it is better to just build a cocoon and then appreciate the new creature that we become. Let's explore the strategy of the caterpillar a bit more, and learn how the Citizens Amendment uses it to help us transform.

A story that continues to have great meaning to me and my family illustrates how this cocoon process works. Many years ago, we took a drive in the mountains to have a cookout with our young son and his friend. We were going to a campground which, on the map, appeared to be two or three miles off the main highway. We arrived at the turnoff, a small dirt road, and began a winding drive.

Time passed and as we had gone five or six miles, my driving became more intense. We had not seen another car in either direction and there were no road signs. I rounded the curves tightly, and everyone became impatient with finding the camp. Eventually, we came upon a car approaching from the opposite direction. We flagged it down and asked the driver how much farther it was to the campground. The answer was a shock—another 18 miles of slow mountain road!

I continued driving, but in our impatience, we did something we later realized was crucial. We stopped the car. We sat for a minute by the side of the road and talked about what we wanted, when we were going to eat, and other concerns. After mulling the situation and examining our feelings, we chose to keep going.

A little farther, on we came upon a beautiful valley and got out for a moment to take a picture. A little farther yet, we discovered an apple tree and the boys brought us each an apple. The impatience that we had been feeling changed to enjoyment and laughter. We arrived at the campground, surprised that the time had gone so fast. Our trip, hurrying tensely to a destination, had been transformed into a beautiful country drive—a creative, enjoyable time.

Prior to stopping the car, there were two choices: keep going or turn around. Stopping the car was a third choice. And from this decision everything changed. It wasn't solving the problem, but the problem got solved anyway.

This third choice is an easy one to forget. There is no adequate word for it, so I call it a *tobe* (rhymes with robe) for "Time **Out: BE**." It is choosing to enter the "zone of transformation," where new options can emerge or where we might more fully become ourselves. In many ways, it is the ultimate choice. Shakespeare's Hamlet asks,

"To be, or not to be? That is the question." Selecting the tobe is choosing "to be," while picking one of the two apparent choices is choosing "not to be," which, for our society, can turn out to be suicidal.

Tobes Invite Transformation

A tobe is a "time out" from trying to make things happen and, instead, making space for self-organizing change. We let go of control, create a safe space, and trust that something new will emerge. It might begin as silence. Or a prayerful attitude. Or it could be transformational talking. But in any case, this third choice is letting go of trying to control things and attending to what is, in a deep and heartfelt way.

It can feel risky. It is stepping outside of the Box system we are in and trusting that Real Life has something to offer. In his book, *Think on These Things*, J. Krishnamurti says, "When you invite life, things begin to happen." Then he adds, "But you see we don't want to invite life, we want to play a safe game; and those who play a safe game die very safely. Is that not so?"

In the last chapter, we saw how regularly-scheduled Choice-creating meetings can facilitate transformation. Through working together on the important issues of the sawmill, the employees became different—more caring, more empowered. But at the same time, because they cared more, it made them vulnerable.

Chart #10 illustrates how these regular tobes establish a self-organizing dynamic of change, a Circle system. The Wisdom Council is a tobe process for the whole system. With it, we take regular moments of time outside of our usual activities to be authentic with one another, to drop our roles, to be open-hearted, and to allow ourselves to become different. It is an annual shared "stopping the

Tobes Transform a System

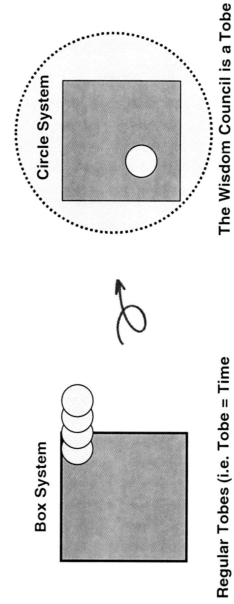

Circle System

Box System

Regular Tobes (i.e. Tobe = Time Out: BE) establish a Circle system and Co-founder culture

The Wisdom Council is a Tobe process that changes the structure and involves everyone

Chart #10

car," where all of us seek clarity about what is really happening and what we really want.

Self-reflection

Just stopping and not acting can allow big changes to happen. It is an emptying of the mind of expectations and patterns which often brings clarity and authenticity. Gandhi reminds us, "In the attitude of silence the soul finds the path in a clearer light, and what is elusive and deceptive resolves itself into crystal clearness."

Once we step out of the old patterns, it's possible to look back and see with new eyes what is happening. New capabilities for change then become available. In *The Inner Game of Tennis*, author Tim Gallway describes a practical example. A business executive came to Tim to improve his backhand. He had been to five different tennis instructors, all of whom told him that he needed to lower his backswing. Knowing this, yet incapable of doing it, the man wanted yet another lesson.

Tim took the man to view his reflection in a nearby window. He had the man stroke an imaginary ball and watch himself. The man exclaimed with genuine surprise, "Hey, I really do take my racket back high! It goes up above my shoulder!" After seeing this, he "got" what the others were saying and naturally adjusted his swing. The problem resolved itself in just a few minutes, with no teaching.

Often our actions, attitudes, and capabilities are stuck because we are living according to a mental image of what is going on, rather than what is really going on. Tobes allow us to let go of that "story" we tell ourselves, and to develop a more accurate description. Then change is easy. We find ourselves naturally feeling, being, and acting differently.

In a personal example of how a new story can change attitudes, I was once helping my young son get ready for bed. He seemed to be in a foul mood, frustrated with everything I did. I was losing patience when my wife said, "Jim, when he is irritable like this, it usually means he is coming down with an illness." This had not occurred to me. We both had the same information, but she had created a different story about what was happening. By adopting her story, I saw my son as needing me, and found myself acting with infinite patience and understanding. Also, since he awakened with a fever the next morning, her story proved to be more accurate.

With regular periods of self-reflection, we can free ourselves from the old stories that captivate us like, "life is a competition," "we can't achieve our goal without more money," "those other people are bad," etc. Tobes provide a way for us to switch out of "hurrying to get somewhere" and, instead, to realize we are on an exciting journey of discovery and adventure.

Wisdom Council Example

A Wisdom Council was recently tried in a farm credit bank. Over a period of a year and a half, the bank held three Wisdom Councils, each of which provided a striking example of how the self-reflective process works in a large system of people. The first step was that a group of managers got turned on to the concept. Then all bank employees were presented with the idea and voted to try it for four cycles over the course of two years. Random numbers were drawn and twelve employees were selected for the first meeting of a day-and-a-half. Participants met and listed a number of issues they might address, and chose as their starting point: "We don't have enough time."

That was the old story. In their meeting, people looked further into this issue and decided that the real issue was, "We aren't forward-looking." Self-reflection revealed that the people of the bank considered themselves to be forward-looking, but everyone had their head down, just trying to keep up with day-to-day activities. It was an old-story of what "work" looks like. The consensus was to change this image of work, because people in a high-quality organization need time to think, learn, and to talk with others. At the conclusion of their meeting, they presented this perspective back to all the employees of the bank and disbanded.

At the second Wisdom Council a few months later, with all new people, someone asked if the first Wisdom Council had made any difference. After a moment of awkward silence, each person spoke, saying it had made a difference to him or her. That is, while each individual knew it had a personal effect for them, they assumed it had little effect on others. One person reported that her work group now begins every meeting by assessing how "forward-looking" they've become. Another reported that being "forward-looking" was a key topic in the recent strategic planning efforts.

This second Wisdom Council went on to develop a different topic: ways to empower bank employees. As their meeting was ending, however, they realized that they weren't on such a different topic after all. They had naturally built on the work of the first Wisdom Council, describing what it meant to be forward-looking. Immediately after their presentation to the rest of the bank, this time everyone met in small groups and discussed the results. This time, a number of movements started, including a newsletter, job partnering with others, getting to know members of the board of directors, learning more about the farm credit system, holding regular luncheon meetings, etc.

The third Wisdom Council meeting five months later was especially striking because, within an hour's time, all employees of the bank changed their story of what was happening. It was a scary time for people because a corporate merger was in the works. All bank activities were going to be relocated and massive layoffs were likely. People were afraid of losing their jobs.

This Wisdom Council chose to address these fears. As they looked into their dire situation, however, they started seeing it differently. Someone described what had happened to him and his coworkers the last time there was a merger. It was a *positive* experience. Others began to appreciate that, if laid off, there would be plenty of lead-time, and they would receive substantial compensation, training, relocation help, and other benefits. These advantages were known already, but the old story about layoffs, that they are bad, still held sway. The session ended enthusiastically, with people seeing the layoffs in positive terms and being excited to present this view to the rest of the bank.

In twenty minutes of presentation, the Wisdom Council described their new perspective to all employees. People broke into small group conversations for another twenty minutes, and then each group reported their conclusion—which was basically that they were in agreement. It was a good deal. In just an hour, the mood at the bank switched from anxiety to enthusiasm. There was a new openness to this take-over. Follow-up luncheons were scheduled for people to keep talking and learning about their options. Afterward a human resources manager told me, "I could never have gotten this positive reaction from people, even if I'd talked to them all day about the benefits."

Normally, it is difficult to change stories. Just try telling smokers who think they enjoy the taste of smoking, for example, about the nature of addictions or about the health risks they take. Frequently, when we are attached to specific behaviors and have bought into a story that justifies them, we resist seeing or hearing what is really going on. But the Wisdom Council provides a way for us to get past our adherence to old stories, to just see what is happening.

As a society, we live within a story about the importance of money. At the same time, most of us know that corporate values and our money-oriented system are destroying the natural wealth of this planet, and even risking the continued success of the human species. The breakthrough answer to this problem may be to collectively stop and think for a moment, and look at what is really going on. Just this, can be transforming.

What We Really Want

In taking a tobe and seeing the situation with new eyes, there is often a shift in values. After we see what is *really* happening, the natural question is, "What do we *really* want?" Asking this question opens the door to transformation.

A conversation I had with a social worker illustrates this shift. There was a job opening in her office and she wanted it, but was worried that she might not get it. She explained to me that she was the most qualified person in her office and felt deserving of the promotion. As she spoke, I could hear a kind of childish whine in her voice, so I asked her what she really wanted. Her response was the same—to be given that supervisory job. I asked the same question again, more strongly, "What do you REALLY want?" After a moment, she paused and took a deep breath. The whine disappeared and her voice became more assertive. She said, "You wouldn't have to pay me to design gardens!"

Clearly, this woman already knew she liked to design gardens. But her answer to the question surprised even her. It was as if some inner voice broke through and spoke to her, as well as to me. I don't know if she eventually made a choice to pursue this field, but I'm sure she didn't pursue the promotion with the same degree of single-mindedness.

Once, for a few months, I conducted an experimental class for seventh and eighth grade children in our local school. Called "In Left Field," it was not really a class, but tobes at the end of the school day, two times a week. There were no learning objectives or lesson plans. I merely facilitated the kids to figure out what they wanted and then helped them get it.

People warned me that the attention span of this age group was about eight minutes, but in the first session I don't think I got that long. One of the boys immediately started banging his hands on his thighs and bouncing in his seat, distracting most everyone. I asked him what he was doing. He didn't know at first, but then excitedly remembered, "I'm playing the rhythm game."

I asked him to show us what he meant. He jumped up and organized everyone. You have probably played this game. Once we got going, I realized I had. Everyone sits in a circle and counts off so each person has a number. Then the group starts beating a rhythm: two hits to the thighs and a snap of the fingers of the left hand, then the right. The whole cycle is repeated like a drum beat. Each time the group snaps their left hand, one person says his or her number. Then, when the right fingers snap, that person says another number. If it's your number, you have to realize it quickly and respond in rhythm next time, saying your number and then another. If you mess up, then you lose, everyone laughs, you go back to the last position, and those behind you move up.

The first class was taken up with this exercise. The boy got everyone playing, the kids were laughing, and before long class was over. From the standpoint of classroom management, the kids just played. But later, I realized that through this tobe process and doing what they wanted, they had taught themselves the lesson which the teachers had told me they most needed: how to concentrate and act in coordination with others. What emerged from their brief moment of self-reflection was both fun and valuable.

Subsequent "classes" developed similarly, with the kids coming into the room and starting something fun. Soon the teachers began reporting that the kids were easier to teach. They were more interested in the topics presented and better behaved in learning them.

This was the same lesson I had learned in the mill, that periodic tobe meetings, where people self-organized and followed their passion, brought changes to the system as a whole. Mill workers and children alike became more authentic, interested, curious, and involved.

Tobes for We the People

The Citizens Amendment is a tobe process for We the People. As a society, we step out of our story about what is going on, to see what is really going on. Then we figure out what we really want.

This kind of tobe has happened before. The three or so days after the assassination of President Kennedy, in November 1963, is one example. His death sparked a national stopping that changed the United States forever. The Civil Rights legislation and poverty programs that immediately followed were a direct result.

The U.S. Constitutional Convention was also a tobe. The Founders feared that the benefits of the revolution against England were about to unravel, and a "stop the car" meeting was convened. The most respected men of that time gathered for four months behind closed doors to self-reflect and think about what was really needed. Most everyone else on the continent, at least the former colonists, paused along with them.

This kind of a national tobe was a new concept that eventually generated a new system of government. The Founders assumed other "times out" would follow. The document they created, the U.S. Constitution, has two clauses which hint at these coming tobes.

The first is in Article II, section 3, which describes the State of the Union message. It says that every so often the president will go to Congress with a self-reflective statement of how things are going. The clause reads: "[The President] shall from time to time give to the Congress information of the State of the Union, and recommend to their consideration such measures as he shall judge necessary and expedient. . . ."

This was a marvelous addition to the Constitution, but it is not quite the tobe it should be. For a democracy, the tobe clause should say, "Each year, We the People will get together to think about how well things are going and reach joint conclusions about what we see and what we want." But, of course, without electronic communication, modern transportation, or innovations in organizational development, the Founders probably couldn't imagine such a possibility. Without the Wisdom Council to generate transformational talking, it would be extremely difficult.

During the Washington and Adams administrations, the State of the Union message was a formal statement. When Jefferson was elected, he didn't appreciate the royal trappings and felt uncomfortable as a speaker. He merely sent Congress a letter, which, for over 100 years, became the way it was done. But with the advent of radio and television, the tobe potential of this constitutionally sanctioned event has increased. Now, there is a chance for everyone to hear the speech and for the president to help everyone self-reflect. Unfortunately, the high powered Game nature of our system has corrupted this. Now it is just one more axe-grinding political speech given by the president, with a "rebuttal" from the party that is out of office.

The second tobe opportunity in the Constitution is in Article V that describes the amendment procedure. The Constitution outlines two ways to propose amendments and two ways to ratify them. The first method of proposing amendments is to hold another constitutional convention. This has never been done, and it is not clear how it would be. But if it were done, it would likely be a tobe. Instead, every proposed amendment has been enacted via the more political path, where both houses of Congress pass the proposal by a two-thirds majority.

Once successfully passed by Congress, an amendment must be ratified by three-fourths of state legislatures or state conventions. So again, the tobe potential in the Constitution can be averted in favor of normal, adversarial politics. Technically, amendments can be added to the Constitution without any involvement of We the People, through the votes of a few thousand elected representatives.

In fact, the last amendment happened with few people even noticing. The Twenty-seventh Amendment says that a pay increase voted by Congress cannot take effect until the following Congress. It was part of the original Bill of Rights of 1789, but hadn't been ratified by enough states. In 1982, Gregory Watson, a student at the University of Texas, recognized that this idea had merit and that it was only a few states away from ratification. He and others lobbied in specific state legislatures and, on May 7, 1992, it became the Twenty-seventh Amendment.

For true democracy to exist, tobes are crucial. We the People should be stepping outside of the Game periodically, reflecting about our situation and determining what we really want. Once we do this, we will start changing the story we tell ourselves about what is going on. Then we'll start seeing with new eyes, being more authentic, feeling more empowered, and finding that we have greater capability for making change. The Citizens Amendment will structure this transformational opportunity at least once a year.

— 14 —

Changing Our Mythology

Myth is the music we dance to even when we cannot name the tune.

Joseph Campbell

As we saw in the last chapter, the stories we tell ourselves about what is happening play a crucial role in our attitudes, capabilities, sense of empowerment—even our health. We've already seen that, by establishing a tobe process, the Citizens Amendment will help us escape from old negative stories and create new positive ones. We live our lives embedded in stories established long before we were born and outside of conscious awareness. Enacting the Citizens Amendment will dramatically affect these stories.

The word "myth" has almost become a synonym for "false." But really, a myth is what's true. It's our "reality." It's only after this view of reality is seen as wrong, that we look back and see an old myth. To the Greeks of the ancient world, for example, the stories about gods on Mount Olympus were how it really was. It's only because we have updated this viewpoint that we now see them as being like fairy tales.

Managing Our Myth

Cultural myths are held in place by symbols, rituals, and roles. We can alter the myths by adjusting these symbolic elements. A simple, yet powerful illustration of how this works struck me one day in 1994, on a trip to Germany with my family. We were visiting a U.S. Army base after the end of the cold war, and the base was being closed. The unit's museum was still open. It was a little hut at the back of the base, and we went in. On display were uniforms and artifacts from soldiers of the Blackhawk Brigade who fought in the Spanish-American War, World War I, and World War II, along with lists of Brigade soldiers who had died.

I noticed an attendant emptying the museum and packing all the paraphernalia into boxes. She explained to me that this brigade was being deactivated, so all materials were being sent to a warehouse in Washington, D.C. They would be stored until the brigade was reactivated. When the boxes are unpacked then, some group of newly-gathered soldiers will be assigned the name "Blackhawk Brigade" and will instantly have a proud history on which to look back.

The army is smart. Not only does it provide an organizational structure, technology, training, comradeship, and incentives, it also empowers soldiers with a mythology, an instant long-lasting relationship by which new recruits can link themselves to an honored tradition.

The U.S. Constitution serves as the crucial, symbolic anchor for one of our key cultural myths. The myth goes something like this: *Our founding "fathers" established a near perfect system. The people of today, especially today's politicians, are not of their caliber. We are more selfish and limited in our reasoning and values. Because of these inadequacies, it is important that we adhere closely to the desires and design of the Founders. It's only because we have drifted away from their design that we have problems today.*

But the Preamble to the Constitution hints at another story, that We the People are both capable and in charge. The Citizens Amendment picks up on this new story and fulfills it. It answers basic questions like, "Who is 'We the People'? How do they meet? What do they talk about? How do they decide matters?" The new story says: *We the People are us—all the ordinary people of today. We are intelligent, wise, and capable of self-governance. We can work together to achieve true democracy, in a thoughtful and virtuous way.*

In his book, *The Frozen Republic: How the Constitution is Paralyzing Democracy*, Daniel Lazare pleads for us to make this shift in our thinking: "Americans must stop thinking of democracy as a gift of the Founders and a gift of the gods, something that allows millions of voices to cry, 'me! me! me!' while politicians and judges divide up the spoils according to some time-honored formula. Rather, they'll have to think of it as an intellectual framework that *they* create and continuously update, one that allows them to tackle the problems of the modern world not as individuals but as a society."

To make this shift in mythology does not mean that our reverence for the Founders and what they have done is diminished in any way. Their heroism will always be part of our story. My favorites are George Washington and James Madison. Somehow, George Washington held the allegiance of a ragtag group of rebels through one defeat after another, against overwhelming odds. It was largely his personal charisma that sustained the first-ever army of free men long enough to beat the greatest military force in the world. In a world of kings and aristocracy, he was revered like a king, but promised to put away his privileged position when the war was over. Reportedly, when King George III of England was told of this pledge, he remarked, "If he does that he is the greatest man alive." George Washington did it.

Later when asked, he was reluctant to return to political life and attend the Constitutional Convention. But his presence was essential for it to work. He finally chose to participate and was unanimously elected as President of the Convention. Imagine any individual today with that kind of support and respect. Through a new model of leadership, not directing the convention, but facilitating it, he enabled this collection of people to generate a radical new proposal for a working republic.

James Madison was another true hero. A self-effacing man of small stature, who recognized the need for a new kind of government, he feared that the American states would gradually decline into chaos and tyranny unless they were brought together in some new way. In 1787, he engineered a convention to attempt to reorganize society. Although the convention was officially for "the sole and express purpose of revising the Articles of Confederation," the old unworkable system, Madison influenced the Convention to disregard this limitation. . With his other Virginia delegates, he wrote the original draft of the Constitution and assured its later acceptance by writing the Federalist Papers. Then he was the prime mover in getting the Bill of Rights passed.

These are only glimpses at two of the Founders. Both distinguished themselves in many other ways as well, including serving as president. But the point is that their heroism and the role of that heroism in our mythology are not diminished by the enactment of the Citizens Amendment. It's just that their heroism no longer eclipses ours. Their specialness no longer makes us commonplace.

Enacting the Citizens Amendment makes it clear that today's problems are for the people of today to solve. We cannot forever aim ourselves toward restoring the Founders' vision of governance. We must create our own. Our problems exist, in large part, because we are stuck in the shadow of these great people. The next step is to fulfill the story started by the Founders, that We the People formed this democracy and that we are continuing to manage it responsibly.

We also live within an even more fundamental story than our cultural mythology. It is the deep mythology that arises unconsciously in all humankind. The myth of the hero, for instance, takes many different forms, but has a certain commonality throughout all ages and in all cultures. Individual forms of this story resonate with people, like a shared dream.

Earlier, we discussed one modern version of the hero myth, the popular movie *Star Wars,* where a young man, specially born with special gifts, overcomes the evil Darth Vader and creates new order in the universe. Another version of this myth is Disney's popular, *The Lion King.* By examining this myth, we can track the progress of that heroic figure, We the People, on our heroic journey.

In the first scenes of *The Lion King,* Simba is a cub, rightful heir to the jungle kingdom. He is happy playing with friends and living under the protection of his larger than life father. Suddenly his father is dead, and Simba has been deceived into thinking he is at fault. Deeply disappointed in himself, he runs away through a desert where he nearly dies. Eventually, he is saved and taken to a new land where he can put his regrets and his past behind him. This new land has the philosophy of Hakuna Matata: no past, no future, no worries! There, Simba settles down to a carefree life where he focuses only on the present, on friends, and on personal happiness.

One night, however, while lying on his back looking at the stars and joking with friends, he is asked, "What are stars?" This chance question sparks a memory of his father, who talked with him once about the same question, and he is overcome with despair.

Simba's mood of depression is a turning point in the story. Although it seems like a worsening of events to him, it opens the door to new possibilities for both Simba and the kingdom. In Simba's absence, his evil uncle has turned the kingdom into a wasteland where everyone suffers. Although Simba is the rightful king, everyone in the kingdom thinks he is dead.

Magically, however, a wise monkey in the old kingdom realizes that Simba is alive when he senses new-found authenticity in Simba's despair. He immediately sets off to retrieve him. But when he arrives, he finds that Simba is unwilling to return. Neither a sense of duty, nor a budding love for an old girlfriend is strong enough for him to reclaim his destiny.

Simba is running from himself, living the Hakuna Matata philosophy, where neither his past nor his future really matters. To help him get over this, the monkey hits him sharply over the head. When Simba complains, the monkey says, "It doesn't matter—it's in the past."

This is another key moment in the story, because Simba then realizes that he can't escape his past and that he cares deeply. He sets off immediately to go make the kingdom right again.

This moment in the hero's journey is where We the People are today. We also had heroic parents and a special birth. We also are living in the philosophy of Hukuna Matata, pursuing shallow values at the expense of our real destiny. We are also holding to a lighthearted story about how things are, rather than feeling the despair our situation warrants. For us to reclaim our rightful role in charge of the system begins with facing our situation. To right what is wrong, we need to enact the Citizens Amendment.

An Ongoing Process

Of course, the Founders never thought that the Constitution would undermine citizen responsibility. Almost before the ink on the Constitution was dry, George Washington wrote to his nephew, "The warmest friends and the best supporters the Constitution has, do not contend that it is free from imperfections; if evil is likely to arise therefrom, the remedy must come hereafter; for in the present moment, it is not to be obtained; and, as there is a Constitutional door open for it, I think the people (for it is with them to Judge) can as they will have the advantage of experience on their Side, decide with as much propriety on the alterations and amendments which are necessary as ourselves. I do not think we are more inspired, have more wisdom, or possess more virtue than those who will come after us."

Thomas Jefferson also spoke of the danger of letting our high regard for the Founders limit our own actions. In a letter he wrote to Samuel Kercheval in 1816, forty years after the Declaration of Independence:

> *Some men look at constitutions with sanctimonious reverence, and deem them like the arc of the covenant, too sacred to be touched. They ascribe to the men of the preceding age a wisdom more than human, and suppose what they did to be beyond amendment. I knew that age well; I belonged to it, and labored with it. It deserved well of its country. It was very like the present but without the experience of the present; and forty years of experience in government is worth a century of book reading; and this they would say themselves, were they to rise from the dead. I am certainly not an advocate for frequent and untried changes in laws and constitutions. I think moderate imperfections had better be born with; because, when once known, we accommodate ourselves to them, and find practical means of correcting their ill effects. But I also know, that laws and institutions must go hand in hand with the progress of the human mind. As that becomes more developed, more enlightened, as new discoveries are made, new truths disclosed, and manners and opinions change with the change of circumstances, institutions must advance also and keep pace with the times. We might as well require a man to wear still the coat which fitted him when a boy, as civilized society to remain ever under the regimen of their barbarous ancestors. . . . Let us . . . [not] weakly believe that one generation is not as capable as another of taking care of itself, and of ordering its own affairs.*

It has become common for people to think and outwardly express that if we just followed the original Constitution, our problems would go away. The opposite is true. The original Constitution has already failed a number of times. It was changed because it had to be.

The first example happened two years after the Constitution was drafted. Ten amendments were required—the Bill of Rights—to protect citizens from their government. Now, of course, these are popularly recognized as part of the original Constitution. But we owe them more to the anti-federalists who resisted the adoption of the Constitution than to those who attended the constitutional convention.

Another example of its failure was the Civil War. Since Article IV, Section 2 of the Constitution required the return of runaway slaves, and Article I, Section 9 established a ban on all interference with the slave trade until 1808, slavery was built into the original Constitution. And because it counted each slave as three-fifths of a person, it gave the slave-holding states a near veto on any attempt to change this. The Civil War was how the Constitution was finally corrected. Immediately afterwards, the victorious North imposed the 14th and 15th Amendments on the South.

Later, there was another failure: the Great Depression. No amendment was added this time, but what the Constitution said was changed nonetheless, because it was interpreted differently. The old view held that government must keep "hands off" the economy. After the economy broke down and people began suffering en masse, the Supreme Court reinterpreted the Constitution to allow an activist, regulatory government to pursue the "general welfare." This change essentially allowed government to begin managing the Game.

The Citizens Amendment is one more instance of meeting a societal crisis with a constitutional adjustment. It's one more step on the hero's journey for We the People. With it, We assume control of our system in a way that all people can participate.

Part V

GOING FORWARD

. . . even the Constitution of the United States needs to be reconsidered and altered—not to cut the federal budget or to embody this or that narrow principle, but to . . . create a whole new structure of government capable of making intelligent, democratic decisions necessary for our survival in a Third Wave, twenty-first-century America.

Alvin and Heidi Toffler, *Creating a New Civilization*

.

— 15 —

The New Common Sense

There is no way we can choose sustainability until we
change our form of governance . . . to a democracy.
We don't have a democracy. We've never had one in
this country. We have less of one now than we've ever
had. We have a government by and for money.

Paul Hawken, *New Dimensions*

*I*n 1776 Tom Paine wrote a pamphlet called *Common Sense*. The ideas in it were crucial to building support for the American Revolution. It was written in the language of ordinary people and spoke plainly about how the normal way of organizing society, with a king and an aristocracy, didn't make sense. He described a different common sense, with a government formed by consent of the people and governed by the rule of law. Although these were popular ideas for intellectuals then, they were actually more heresy than common sense. His book laid the groundwork for this different common sense to take hold.

The aim of *Society's Breakthrough!* is similar to what Paine had in mind. Here, we discuss how our current common sense, emphasizing Game values, debate, competition for survival, adversarial politics, etc., no longer works, and consider how to adopt the next one. As a culture, we cannot thrive, or even survive, if we continue thinking the old way. As in Paine's time, we must have a common sense more consistent with the reality of our situation, and with the latest developments of science. Today's new-science includes quantum mechanics, chaos theory, and evolutionary biology, which support the participative, evolutionary perspective of the Circle culture, in the same way that the linear, orderly perspective of eighteenth century science supported the Box culture.

Many people are already trying out the new common sense in aspects of their lives. Attempting to live according to Circle values, they feel responsible for the planet, seek consensus, and look within to know what is right. They want thoughtful, respectful conversations, not debate. They want to include everyone, not just people like themselves. They want to face the big issues, not avoid them. And they want to be creative as well as rational, not just the knee-jerk implementation of more laws. But how to make the shift?

For Paine, the answer to this question was clear. His pamphlet advocated that people take action to separate from England. It wasn't enough for them to just think differently. There had to be concrete steps, like declaring independence, fighting for it, and structuring a new kind of society. Today we have a much easier job. We just have to enact a low risk amendment to the U.S. Constitution, one that gives us the chance to stop and think, and facilitates us to become We the People.

The Old Common Sense

When I talk with people in a quiet moment away from the hustle and bustle of everyday, most seem to know and accept that our system isn't working—not for society as a whole, and not for them personally.

To make a living we compromise ourselves in so many ways, working more hours than we'd like, buying more stuff than we need, having less time for ourselves and those we love, and making political choices that do not begin to reflect what we really want or what is needed. The system encourages us to not pay attention to what it is doing or to our deepest values, but to get caught up in the superficial Game, and the pursuit of mindless material growth.

As Robert E. Lane says in *Loss of Happiness in Market Democracies*, "Amidst the satisfaction people feel with their material progress, there is a spirit of unhappiness and depression haunting advanced market democracies throughout the world. . . . The haunting spirit is manifold; a postwar decline in the United States in people who report themselves as happy, a rising tide in all advanced societies of clinical depression and dysphoria (especially among the young), increasing distrust of each other and of political and other institutions, declining belief that the lot of the average man is getting better, a tragic erosion of family solidarity and community integration together with an apparent decline in warm, intimate relations among friends."

Beyond these effects on us are the startling statistics of our dire ecological situation. In *The Last Hours of Ancient Sunlight*, Thom Hartmann says that every twenty-four hours, there are 200,000 fewer acres of rain forest, 13 million more tons of toxic chemicals are released, 45,000 more people die of starvation, and 130 plant or animal species become extinct.

Business entrepreneur and author, Paul Hawken, summarizes the situation: "We live in a time in which every living system is in decline, and the rate of decline is accelerating as our economy grows. The commercial processes that bring us the kind of lives we supposedly desire are destroying the earth and the life we cherish. . . . We are losing our forests, fisheries, coral reefs, topsoil, water, biodiversity, and climatic stability. The land, sea, and air have been functionally transformed from life-supporting systems into repositories for waste. Feeling the momentum of loss at the beginning of a new century, one wants to close one's eyes. Yet that is the very thing that will bring forth ruin."

No one wants what we are bringing about, yet we are all complicit in bringing it about. Struggling to grasp this reality one night, I asked my wife, Jean, "What does it mean that we live in a non-sustainable society?" She didn't have a response, but the next morning she shared a dream that answered my question. In her dream, the fathers in our neighborhood couldn't agree on something, so they killed each others' sons. The overwhelming thought for her in this dream was that, as this group of men was unable or unwilling to come together and find a way through their problem, the outcome became the deaths of our children. Isn't this what we are doing on a global scale?

In his book, *Requiem for Modern Politics*, William Ophuls says, "It comes down to this: modern civilization has no future. It confronts the same lethal combination of ecological collapse and inner decay that has extinguished previous civilizations. . . . only a new and radically different philosophy of governance can foster the wisdom and virtue that are indispensable for both the felicity of the individual and for the peace, welfare and justice of the community."

The New Common Sense

These problems would begin to be resolved if the Circle structure were in place. Then it would be common sense to acknowledge them, face them, and get creative about solving them. Tom Paine knew about this more modern common sense and referred to it as "society" instead of "government." He didn't focus on it in his writings though, because he thought it was impossible to achieve it in a large system. In *Common Sense* he said:

> *Society in every state is a blessing, but government even in its best state is but a necessary evil in its worst state an intolerable one. . . .*

In order to gain a clear and just idea of the design and end of government, let us suppose a small number of persons settled in some sequestered part of the earth, unconnected with the rest, they will then represent the first peopling of any country, or of the world. In this state of natural liberty, society will be their first thought. . . .

Thus necessity, like a gravitating power, would soon form our newly arrived emigrants into society, the reciprocal blessings of which, would supersede, and render the obligations of law and government unnecessary while they remained perfectly just to each other. . . .

But as the colony increases, the public concerns will increase likewise, and the distance at which the members may be separated, will render it too inconvenient for all of them to meet on every occasion as at first, when their number was small, their habitations near, and the public concerns few and trifling. This will point out the convenience of their consenting to leave the legislative part to be managed by a select number chosen from the whole body, who are supposed to have the same concerns at stake which those have who appointed them, and who will act in the same manner as the whole body would act were they present. . . .

Here then is the origin and rise of government; namely, a mode rendered necessary by the inability of moral virtue to govern the world; here too is the design and end of government, viz. freedom and security.

The main thing holding us back from a reliance on the Circle system, or what Paine calls "society," is that the Box structure constrains us to a reliance on "government." The Citizens Amendment releases us from this constraint and promotes a reliance on our natural wisdom and virtue—as individuals and all of us together. The Amendment promises changes to both our system and us.

Clearly, we should be talking creatively about the important issues we face. That is certainly commonsensical. The hang up is most people don't think it's possible that ordinary people can be wise, nor that large numbers of people can hold a conversation, nor that transformational talking can be guaranteed. But with the Citizens Amendment these would happen.

Once we are talking open-mindedly and open-heartedly, we will discover that breakthrough solutions already exist for most of the overwhelming problems we face. What we lack is a way to consider them and to act on them. The book, *Natural Capitalism: Creating the Next Industrial Revolution,* by Paul Hawken, Amory Lovins, and L. Hunter Lovins, enumerates many ways to adapt capitalism to our ecological troubles. David Korten's book, *The Post Corporate World: Life After Capitalism* and Janine M. Benyus' *Biomimicry: Innovation Inspired by Nature* provide other sets of solutions. We are not at a loss for workable solutions. We just need a way to consider them properly and to build the political will to implement them.

Structure Is Key

As people experiment with the new Circle common sense and appreciate its potential, they often seek to transform society through education, electing facilitative leaders, changing the laws, or joining with others in local actions. They imagine that if enough people could become conscious, change their attitudes, and start living differently, a critical mass will be reached and the system will shift. Or, they imagine that if enough people could meet in small groups to pray and meditate on this necessary change, the best human values will take charge. While these efforts are crucial to bringing about the Circle culture, by themselves they cannot succeed. The overriding presence of the Game structure remains dominant and ultimately frames how we think—enforcing transactional talking and determining the actions we take.

Even if we were to successfully influence everyone to adopt Circle values, we would still trash our planet. Our political system would still work through special interest proposals and majority voting. Large organizations driven by measurable results would still control most people's means to a livelihood, direct their energies, and allocate resources. The tragedy of the commons would still be in place. And profit-oriented organizations would still control the media, tell us what we know, and shape us to serve their corporate clients.

At a conference recently, I saw an interesting example of how structure affects the results of a system despite the efforts of individuals within it. I was in a small group of educated, aware, and concerned people. They were discussing environmental problems and how to turn them around. There was a tone of deep communion and all were settled into the spirit of reflection and reverence. They had made personal decisions to simplify their own lives and most thought that these individual actions and this collective spirit were the missing ingredients for solving society's problems.

We started talking about how to spread this attitude and spirit beyond the room into the world. One person suggested an idea. After a moment, someone else pointed out some limitations to the idea and mentioned another one. Others made additional comments and criticisms, and soon there was a debate. In no time, this collection of conscious people was approximating special interest politics and heading toward a compromise decision that no one could get excited about.

They were aware people, maybe the best you could hope for. Only, the structure of the meeting aimed them toward decision-making, not Choice-creating, and they were stuck in that dynamic. Each person was trying to influence others to his or her position.

A Dynamic Facilitator would've made the needed difference. Then people could have said what came to their minds and, their ideas would have been received by all and benefited the group, rather than sparking arguments.

This is what the Citizens Amendment would do for society. By changing the structure of how we think and talk, it would positively affect all the important problems we face.

A Global Solution

At this point, you might be concerned that the Citizens Amendment is only a national strategy, while the most significant problems we face are global. There are many ways, however, that the Amendment would have global impact.

Earlier in *Chapter 6 — The Wisdom Council and Whole-system Resonance,* we discussed five ways by which a small group of people assembled into a Wisdom Council will generate the involvement of an entire system of people. At the time, we considered these factors from only the perspective of the American system. But, except for one—that world's people could not directly participate in this Wisdom Council—all other factors would still apply, generating whole-system involvement throughout the world.

A new amendment of this nature will be big news. Because of American wealth, power, and global influence, the people and governments of other nations watch most everything we do with close attention, some with favor and some with dread. As the Wisdom Councils' Statements take effect, many would watch with renewed hope as we more fully embody the principles of fairness and justice that we profess.

As they see the Wisdom Council being successful in helping us, other countries may become interested in adopting it as well; not only long-time republics, but also those still grappling with the meaning of self-governance.

For their own reasons, other countries may act first to adopt Wisdom Councils. South Africa may adopt this process as a way to overcome its massive crime problem and help it successfully integrate blacks and whites, or Great Britain to help it find a democratic replacement for the House of Lords and overcome its overt class structure, or Canada as a way to find just solutions to native claims and the Quebec separatist movement, or a Middle Eastern country to create a safe way to become more democratic.

Wisdom Councils may also be used to help solve "impossible" conflicts like the Israeli-Palestinian issue. For example, if each side of this conflict had a Wisdom Council, then there could be a wise and reasonable voice of the Israeli people, speaking directly with a wise and reasonable voice of the Palestinian people. It would generate a different kind of "negotiation," people to people rather than government to government. One way or the other, because it is so needed, cities, nations, and organizations throughout the world will begin to use Wisdom Councils.

As people are exposed to the Choice-creating conversations of Wisdom Councils, they will hear ordinary folk talk about important issues with passion, creativity, and wisdom. If Choice-creating is then taken up in these lands, we will take giant steps forward in global consciousness.

An exciting possibility is that we might eventually establish a global Wisdom Council, with 24 ordinary people chosen at random from the world's total population. What an exciting vision for how people of all races, cultures, and religions might really create a world that works for all!

Until then, an American Wisdom Council will have special symbolic significance throughout the world. It would be like the signing of the Magna Carta by King John of England in 1215. In that case, the barons of England forced their king to acknowledge the rule of law, while simultaneously legitimizing the *concept* of the rule of law for all people. Similarly today, all constitutional "democracies" rely on We the People of the United States, as a world-symbol of self-governance. Just as these nations didn't need to reinvent the rule of law, they also did not reformulate a We the People. Instead, they built on the preexisting notion of a wise and responsible We the People established in 1787. To form their nations they convened a committee of experts and advisors to draft a constitution, which the people could vote on, yes or no.

Even Great Britain, whose history holds the roots of Western democracy, symbolically depends on the American We the People. Its history has no such defining moment when the people asserted power. There is just a centuries-old tug-of-war between the monarch and a determined elite who, bit by bit, wrests power away from the monarch, giving some to the common people. Today, for example, a person entering military service in Great Britain still swears allegiance, not to the people or to a constitution, but to the monarch.

Adding the Citizens Amendment to the United States Constitution reconvenes this vital world-symbol, We the People. With its multicultural population and already being on center stage, a Wisdom Council in the United States would be a kind of microcosm within a microcosm.

That is, we in the United States are in the midst of a brief "butterfly moment." Like our Founders, we have been presented with the rare opportunity to act positively in a way that will reverberate throughout history. This moment of high leverage for global impact won't last long, so we must act soon.

The New Conversation

The advent of the Box system brought freedom, new levels of social justice, the spirit of entrepreneurship, and material success to many. At the same time, there are growing indicators that our system is failing. The terrorist actions of September 11, 2001 have served notice that deep discontent exists, that we are at risk, and that fundamental change is needed. Other crises are brewing: increased school violence, the suppression of civil liberties, the deterioration of the environment, the obscene concentration of wealth, weapons of mass destruction, and the rise of Triangle-like fundamentalist movements. The image of the sudden and surprising collapse of the burning World Trade Center towers may be an accurate metaphor for the way a global system collapses.

In today's terrorist-obsessed times, none of us feels as safe as we once did. Much of the blame for this threat has been laid on the hate and frustration that impoverished people often have for the dominant system. Someone said it beautifully, "Violence is the expression of impotence grown unbearable."

By enacting the Citizens Amendment, we uncover new options for addressing this issue and its causes. It provides us with what we need most—the potential for breakthroughs of trust.

The horrible acts of September 11, 2001 killed many people. But killing people was not the primary aim of the terrorists. More fundamentally they were making a statement as part of some large global conversation, and insisting on being heard. They were protesting the dominance of the American system by lashing out at its most visible symbols, the World Trade Center and the Pentagon. They were saying "no" to the Box system and the Game mentality in favor of the Triangle system and the Loyalist mentality.

Our response to their "statement" in this "conversation" has mostly been through government actions and public relations. However, with the Citizens Amendment, we provide ourselves with more options. Most importantly, we reshape the nature of the overarching "conversation." We provide a way by which we can listen and speak to the people of the world, from the heart as well as the head.

The Citizens Amendment will facilitate new conversations that are creative and aimed at solving real issues. It will provide us with new ways to heal the trauma of terrorist acts and threats. Ultimately, because it will transform our system from the Box to the Circle, it will remove the key source of anger and frustration for those who become terrorists: the unfairness and materialism of the Game-system and how it dominates them.

Until now, Americans have lived in a protected environment, as if we've had high walls around us. But in a world where small groups and individuals are technologically empowered with the latest weaponry to wreck havoc if they want to, our geographical seclusion and military might will no longer deliver the security we desire. To gain that we must have a breakthrough in trust.

But, to try and maintain the Box system in the face of growing interdependence and inequities means reduced trust, lessening freedoms, fewer resources, more crises, and more danger. We don't want that path. The smart path is to enact the Citizens Amendment and to start the new conversation, with everyone involved.

Willis Harman, former President of the Institute of Noetic Sciences said in a talk to the Foundation for Global Community, "I've come to believe that global dialogue is really the source of the change force that is going to bring the modern era to a close and bring us into the new era . . ." He's right. We must assure that this global dialogue happens in a way that builds trust, celebrates differences, and respects life.

This book began with the question, "What is fundamentally the most significant problem we face as a society?" No matter what answer you gave, I promised a capital "B" Breakthrough, an answer that would bring important progress to your issue. The Citizens Amendment is that Breakthrough. I hope you agree that this promise has been kept. The next step is up to you. I invite you to seize the opportunity to become a Co-founder of the new society, to share these ideas with others, to practice Dynamic Facilitation and Choice-creating, to initiate Wisdom Councils in your organizations, and to help enact the Citizens Amendment.

Part VI

APPENDICES

We have frequently printed the word democracy. Yet I can not too often repeat that it is a word the real gist of which still sleeps, quite unawakened, not withstanding the resonance and the many angry tempests out of which its syllables have come, from pen or tongue. It is a great word whose history has yet to be enacted.

Walt Whitman

− A −

Frequently Asked Questions

Be patient with all that is unresolved in your heart.
And try to love the questions themselves.

Rainer Maria Rilke

1. *What is Society's Breakthrough?*
It is the Citizens Amendment to the U.S. Constitution which says:

Each year twenty-four registered voters will be randomly selected in a lottery to form a Citizens Wisdom Council. This Wisdom Council will be a symbol of the people of the United States. It will meet for one week to choose issues, talk about them, and determine consensus statements. To ensure creative conversation and unanimous conclusions, the meetings are aided by a facilitator. At the end of the week, the Wisdom Council will present the statements to the nation in a new ceremony, from "We the People" to the people. The Citizens Wisdom Council will then disband permanently and the next year a new Wisdom Council will be randomly selected.

2. Why do we need this Breakthrough?

We are on an unsustainable path that, for it to be corrected, requires a shift in global consciousness. The Citizens Amendment is a low risk, low cost way to facilitate this shift.

3. Why is a constitutional amendment necessary?

Only through an amendment can a "We the People" form and speak with one voice. Anything less creates something that is subservient to government, corporations, and the Constitution. With the Citizens Amendment, we empower ourselves to take charge of the system and begin true democracy.

4. Shouldn't we try this first in local governments or corporations, then build up to the national level?

Yes. Wisdom Councils can and should be applied to states, cities, counties, high schools, corporations, housing projects, labor unions, and any large organization seeking democratic governance. There should be many experiments so that people build confidence in the process. But an amendment to the U.S. Constitution is ultimately essential. Only then have we changed the system to respond to today's reality, and opened the door to a shift in global consciousness.

5. How can twenty-four people represent a huge population like the nation?

Some confuse the Wisdom Council with a poll, where the number of people who are randomly selected must be large enough to be statistically significant. The Wisdom Council is not a poll. It is a symbol, like the flag or the president. The statistical concept of sample size is irrelevant.

6. What if a random selection somehow yields an unrepresentative sample?

Because it is a lottery, it is possible that a particular Wisdom Council will not accurately reflect society. It is unlikely, but possible. The probability of having all women or all men on the Council, for instance, is less than 3 in 10,000,000. But even if there were an unrepresentative group one year, it would not be a problem.

Unanimity is still required, the conversation is still a creative process and, most importantly, the Wisdom Council has no coercive power. If a particular Council says something with which many people in the general population disagree, these Statements will still stimulate crucial dialogue, but will not attract the near-total degree of public support necessary to generate action.

7. *What if insane or chemically-addicted, or the "wrong" people get on the Council?*

Each Wisdom Council is a microcosm of society. Over time alcoholics, drug addicts, racists, and emotionally handicapped people will be selected to serve on Wisdom Councils, in proportion to their percentage in society. But the quality of conversation in the Wisdom Council is different from normal politics. It's "Choice-creating" instead of "decision-making," which even works with people who seem not to be functional.

Yet, even if everything were to fall apart in a worse case scenario, and the Wisdom Council did not reach a consensus that year, it would still spark a larger, creative dialogue.

8. *What is "Choice-creating"? How can a diverse group be expected to reach consensus, or unanimity?*

Choice-creating is a non-judgmental, heart-felt, energy-driven, creative thinking process in which people seek to invent new options that work for everyone. Instead of negotiating agreement on particular points or discussing ideas back and forth, people seek breakthroughs that everyone can fully support. These breakthroughs come in two forms—changes of mind and changes of heart.

Because the conversation process within a Wisdom Council is Choice-creating, not decision-making, and because the Wisdom Council is free to define the problem in its own terms, unanimity can easily be attained.

9. What is a Dynamic Facilitator?

A Dynamic Facilitator is one who has learned to help people think and talk creatively and open-mindedly, using Choice-creating instead of decision-making. He or she does not participate in the conversation, but only supports how the conversation proceeds.

10. What controls are on the facilitator?

An Oversight Committee of former Wisdom Council members chooses facilitators and helps assure capable facilitation. The Wisdom Council can use majority voting to decide whether or not to replace facilitators.

11. How would this small group affect the whole system? Why not involve more people?

The goal of the Wisdom Council is to involve everybody. There are many ways this happens including: a) each registered voter will have a chance to be selected each year; b) all of us will be able to watch most of the dialogues on television, identifying with some of the participants; c) the conclusions reached by the Wisdom Council will be presented back to all of us in a new ceremony; d) we will be invited to dialogue and to discuss the Wisdom Council's conclusions; e) the Wisdom Council symbolizes all of us; f) at times, the Wisdom Council may suggest something for us to do.

Twenty-four is suggested because it is large enough to guarantee diversity, yet small enough for a "small group process." It allows each person plenty of time to express his or her perspective and to play an active role in developing the results.

12. How will the results of the Wisdom Council get translated into action?

We the People already have ultimate responsibility for our system and ultimate power for action. We just don't have a way to use our power responsibly. The Citizens Amendment provides that way.

The Wisdom Council is *not* an advisory group to Congress, hoping they will take action. It is a symbol of all of us, making statements of what we want. If most citizens identify with its

Statements, We the People can act strongly. Together, we have more power than special interest groups, the president, Congress, more even than the U.S. Constitution.

13. *Why not give the Wisdom Council some coercive power?*

If the Citizens Amendment were to give coercive powers to the Wisdom Council, its "real" power would be reduced, not enhanced. Adding coercive power would merely adjust the current, power-based system rather than facilitate its transformation—with higher levels of respect, trust, community, morality, empathy, etc. This kind of change cannot be coerced.

14. *People don't care about politics. Won't they just ignore the Wisdom Council?*

People appear to be apathetic because the current political conversation doesn't involve them in a meaningful way. But they do care about society and societal issues. In fact, they long to engage one another and talk about these issues creatively. The people who don't vote probably would if they thought it meant something.

15. *Won't special interest groups co-opt this process?*

The Wisdom Council is the solution to this problem. It's a way to articulate a powerful *general* interest perspective that can stand up to special interests.

If need be, those selected can be easily kept isolated from outside contact, like a jury.

16. *Why does the Wisdom Council meet for such a short time?*

It is important that the Wisdom Council be comprised of ordinary people—not officials, celebrities, or representatives. If the period is too long, Wisdom Council members become public "personalities" and people will stop identifying with them. Most everyone selected can take one week out of their schedule to attend, and that is plenty of time to address key issues and reach consensus.

17. *How would the Wisdom Council receive expert information? Would they meet with elected officials?*

Since the Wisdom Council is We the People, it can ask the president, officials, or any expert to meet with them. It has no power to force compliance, however. An Oversight Committee comprised of former Wisdom Council members can make the arrangements.

18. *Why don't we link everyone through a computer network, instead?*

Computer networking and web pages are well suited to supporting the Wisdom Council, but are incapable, by themselves, of establishing the essential heart-felt, transformational conversation and coherent voice of the people.

19. *Won't the Citizens Amendment affect just the United States? What about the rest of the world?*

Although an amendment to the U.S. Constitution ostensibly affects only the United States, there are many ways its effect would be global. The topics of conversation, the quality of dialogue and the conclusions that are reached will receive media attention throughout the world. Transnational companies, other countries, and regions like Europe or Latin America may want to use Wisdom Councils to address their "impossible" problems. One day there may even be a World Wisdom Council.

20. *Won't it take forever to get an amendment to the U.S. Constitution enacted?*

The Citizens Amendment is on a fast track compared with other proposed big changes or amendments. There are a number of reasons why it should happen fairly quickly:

• Instituting the Citizens Amendment will allow us to solve urgent problems that seem intractable.

• The Wisdom Council can be tried on a smaller scale—cities, professional organizations, unions, churches, and counties—to solve problems at these levels. Whenever one is tried, within a very short time, the people of that system will have direct experience with its benefits and can envisage how it would work as an amendment.

• Wherever a Wisdom Council is tried, it will be covered by the media. It is well suited to media coverage because it addresses issues people really care about, it happens on center stage for that area so it already has the public's attention, it produces a final result, and it encourages people to engage the media by writing letters to the editor, for instance. The national media will cover any large city that tries it.

• There will be unofficial experiments with national Wisdom Councils. National magazines, TV networks, and/or nonprofit organizations will convene panels modeled on the Wisdom Council, and publicize them and their results.

Society's Breakthrough!

— B —
Experiments and Inquiries

[Global mind change] is largely a matter of people recalling that no matter how powerful the economic or political or even military institution it persists because it has legitimacy, and that legitimacy comes from the perceptions of people. People give legitimacy and they can take it away.

Willis Harman

Before we can enact the Citizens Amendment, we must first test the Wisdom Council in various settings. As described in *Chapter 6 — The Wisdom Council and Whole-system Resonance*, it has twelve essential ingredients.

1. *The Wisdom Council is chartered by the people.*
2. *It is a microcosm of randomly selected people.*
3. *It is empowered to select and frame the issues it addresses.*
4. *The members are chosen in a ceremony: a lottery.*
5. *It is non-coercive.*
6. *It operates in a fishbowl.*

7. *It is dynamically facilitated.*
8. *It generates unanimous statements.*
9. *The results are presented in a ceremony.*
10. *Small group dialogues are convened.*
11. *The process is ongoing.*
12. *The process operates in parallel with normal governance structures.*

As of this writing, there has been only one Wisdom Council that employed all twelve ingredients. It was established by the employees of AgAmerica/Western Farm Credit Banks and was described in *Chapter 13 — Choosing to BE.* Although wildly successful, it ended prematurely through a merger. There have also been a number of other Wisdom Council experiments using most, but not all of the twelve ingredients. In all cases, the process worked more effectively than imagined.

Some of the experiments are described below, along with lessons they teach and questions they raise. From reading about them, you will gain more understanding of the Wisdom Council, especially how it might work for you. I hope you will feel motivated to pursue implementing one in your organization or locality. Doing so would not only be serving that group, but would also spread awareness of these concepts and help transform society.

Background

When I first started proposing the Citizens Amendment to people, I was fairly certain that something like it must have been tried before. I found two examples that deserve attention.

Citizens Juries were mentioned earlier. Here, an organization like the League of Women Voters, defines an issue, such as evaluating available healthcare proposals and choosing the best one. Then, a stratified random sample from the larger population is conducted to assemble a group of twenty-four to reflect certain aspects of the community from which they are drawn, e.g. same age, gender, education, etc. Then this group visits with experts on all sides of the issue, discusses the options, and eventually votes.

One of the exciting lessons to be learned from this work is how responsible these groups of randomly selected people are and how readily transformational dialogue arises in these settings. That is, in tobe-like settings, ordinary Americans do rise to the occasion. They do care. They are good-hearted, and competent, and work toward what is best for all.

William Raspberry (*The Washington Post*, January 23, 1993) reports about one: "These men and women were a microcosm of America, representing the whole range of class, age and regional imperatives that make fair budgeting so difficult. But when they undertook a responsibility that went beyond their individual group interests—when they informed themselves and tried to deal rationally with the national interest—they managed a surprising degree of consensus. There are lessons in that—including the obvious one that this Citizen Jury has done what the Founding Fathers intended Congress to do."

Another approximation of the Wisdom Council was conducted in July 1991 by the editors of the Canadian magazine, *Macleans*. They hired a polling firm to interview and carefully select twelve citizens, one from each of twelve carefully identified patterns of thought. These people were gathered at a resort for three days to create a vision of "The Future of Canada." Roger Fisher, co-author of the popular book *Getting to Yes* was brought in to facilitate, along with other members of the Harvard Negotiation Project.

Over a long weekend, this panel negotiated with one another to reach agreement on a set of conclusions. The story of that weekend and its results were then presented in a television show and written up in a 39-page section of the magazine. The experiment demonstrated, once again, that diverse people can come together and generate unanimity in a remarkably short time.

In this case, those selected were chosen because they represented particular viewpoints, so the eventual results had the flavor of a negotiated contract. Nevertheless, they reached unanimity on specific points aimed at individual Canadians, schoolteachers, non-governmental agencies, provincial governments, the federal government, and the media. The group made recommendations on the economy and suggested changes to the Canadian Constitution. In general, they sought better representation, fairer administration of social programs, and an overall reassessment of how decisions should get made.

In the end, each participant was deeply moved by the experience, and the process generated interest from other Canadians. Hopefully, some national magazine, television network, or philanthropic foundation in the United States will similarly sponsor a national experiment with the Wisdom Council that is ongoing.

Early Experiments

The first experiments with the Wisdom Council happened with employee teams in the sawmill of Simpson Timber Company (Korbel, CA). These meetings, described earlier in *Chapter 12 — "Turning On" Our System,* were instrumental in transforming the management style of the mill over a three year period.

The next experiments with the Wisdom Council were within the *Dynamic Facilitation Skills* seminars. Rather than just organizing participants into small groups to identify issues and practice Dynamic Facilitation, I asked them to pretend they were randomly selected groups charged with creating unanimous statements for the people of the United States.

These simulations uncovered a crucial learning—that Wisdom Councils should focus on solving problems rather than creating statements. Choice-creating is key. If groups focus on rearranging the words of sentences, their creativity is muted and they get into decision-making rather than Choice-creating. But if they devote their energy to tackling real issues and seeking breakthroughs, they are more likely to generate rapid consensus, to build empowerment, and to gain whole-system resonance.

A High School Experiment

One experiment was organized by my son, Dan, as a senior project in his high school. Attendance cards for all students were mixed into one pile and sixteen names were drawn. The sixteen were then invited to participate in three two-hour meetings during one week at an off-campus location. At the end of the third meeting, the mayor, the principal, and the superintendent came for a presentation. The event was covered by the local newspaper.

The sessions began with the facilitator asking, "What are some of the issues we might address?" The students selected their most important one: "School is boring."

Once they started talking and each person had provided his or her purge solution, a breakthrough in awareness occurred. They discovered that there are two kinds of boring: 1) because things go too slowly, and 2) because things go too fast. After this realization, the tone of the conversation changed dramatically. The students started asking questions, learning more about the problem from one another, and seeking answers that would help.

At the end of the three sessions, they reached consensus that class sizes should be smaller; that there needed to be more emphasis on creative learning; that there needed to be a more respectful school environment for both teachers and students; and, that students should take on more responsibility and have more choice in what they learn, and particularly in deciding their own schedules.

All along, the students knew that, immediately following their last meeting, they would make a presentation. Of course, they should've been presenting their results to the whole student body, but that wasn't possible to arrange in this situation. Nevertheless, the scheduled presentation was a powerful motivator to the group.

They organized themselves, with each student presenting one portion of the results. Their recommendations were unanimous, so as each student spoke, he or she felt supported by the whole group and spoke with confidence. They told the story of where they started, how their thinking changed, and where they finally ended up. When they finished, the principal and superintendent enthusiastically exclaimed, "This is great! We've got to keep these kids together!" Their response was gratifying to hear, but it missed the point. It's not that this particular group was so special, but that, with a Wisdom Council process in place, *all* kids could similarly demonstrate their specialness.

This experiment was missing important elements. There was little official involvement by the rest of the school in deciding to try the process, in selecting Wisdom Council members, or in hearing the results, and there was no official opportunity for whole-system dialogue. But even without these, the process generated interest from all sectors of the student body. Even the cynical kids who gather off campus to smoke and make fun of those who participate in student council and other programs were interested. One of them had been selected for the Wisdom Council, so this group was drawn into talking about the same topics as the rest of the campus.

The big learning was to glimpse the immense potential of the Wisdom Council process within high schools. It offers a new way to involve the whole student body, faculty, and community in the education process. It offers a new way to overcome cliques and the threat of school violence. It offers the potential for transforming the education process from a bureaucratic exercise, driven by rigid curricula and standardized testing, to being driven by the students' natural curiosity and passion for learning.

Strategic Leadership Forum Roundtable

In May 1999, another Wisdom Council experiment was arranged within a professional organization, the *Strategic Leadership Forum.* The organizer of the event was Marilyn Norris, editor of the journal *Strategy and Leadership.*

The plan was to invite a random group of association members to meet just prior to the annual conference and report their findings to the conference. However, the finances of the association were perilous, so the scope of the project was scaled back at the last minute.

In the end, a select group of members was assembled from a cross-section of industries. They met the day before the conference to discuss the role of business in the twenty-first century. They reached consensus statements and their results were published in the magazine.

Consensus was reached on many issues including, the increasing pace of change and a concern about lack of jobs in the future; the globalization of business and the need to account for an expanding set of stakeholders; a conflict between Industrial Age values and the new Knowledge Age values, which is affecting how decisions get made and how people are managed. They determined that business must adopt a new role, one where global, social, and environmental issues are just as important as profits. (See *Strategy and Leadership,* Volume 27, July/Aug/September 1999.)

The experiment showed that the Wisdom Council process can work within associations and membership organizations. The group reached thoughtful consensus in the available time, but key factors were missing that limited whole-system involvement—especially the formal presentation and follow-up dialogue opportunities.

Unfortunately, before the magazine story had time to have its impact, the association folded for lack of funds.

Televised Experiment in a City

During this period, I was trying to interest my town's City Council to endorse a two-year trial of the Wisdom Council. I arranged a demonstration event where eight citizens were randomly selected for a two-hour meeting on local access television. The City Council proposed the hottest local issue to this group: Whether or not chain stores should be allowed to locate in town.

The point of the demonstration was to show: 1) that randomly selected people would choose to participate; 2) that they are generally knowledgeable; 3) that a high quality of conversation (Choice-creating) can be assured; 4) that some form of consensus can be reached in a short time; and 5) that the final consensus will be "wise."

The experiment worked. Those selected did choose to come, they did choose the hot topic which the city council proposed, and the group did reach wise consensus rapidly. They said:

1) That the town should preserve its desirable, special qualities and articulate a vision of that specialness.

2) From this vision, clear standards should be set for businesses to ensure the realization of the vision, and to grow it forward. In particular, the historic district of the town should be carefully protected.

3) We should emphasize to townspeople that, just by how they spend money, they vote on which businesses they want to keep in town. But, at the same time, the Wisdom Council pointed out, that those with low or fixed income may not feel so free to exercise this choice.

4) Finally, the Wisdom Council acknowledged that these three steps may not be enough to preserve the unique qualities

of the town. They also tossed out other ideas but did not have time to consider them adequately, such as separately chartering businesses, holding polls to clarify citizen perspectives, enacting special tariffs, or spending tax dollars to support desired businesses.

The event taught some important lessons. Although participants and many in the television audience were excited and enthused about the demonstration, there were others in the audience who found the show difficult to watch. They were not used to Choice-creating. Having the facilitator follow and encourage the energy and passion of the participants made it seem "out of control" to them, especially when people with "wrong" views got to express them and be heard.

After it worked so well, I was expecting the City Council to be pleased, but found to my surprise that they felt threatened. One of its members stated strongly, "We are the Wisdom Council!" The lesson for me was an old one: this is a Breakthrough. It takes some time for people to get comfortable with the idea.

Low Income People's Wisdom Council

One concern that many people raise about a Wisdom Council of randomly selected people is, *what happens when you get someone who is ignorant, someone on drugs, an alcoholic, or someone mentally unstable?* This point is well taken because much of the testing of Choice-creating and Dynamic Facilitation has been in companies or organizations with people who have jobs. How well would it work with those who have difficulty holding jobs, for instance?

One experiment with the Wisdom Council was set up by Adin Rogovin in Eugene, Oregon. The concept was to randomly select people from a pool of welfare recipients in Lane County (Oregon) and gather them for a weekend meeting. They would be dynamically facilitated to create unanimous statements that would be presented to mainstream taxpayers.

The seventeen people who were selected were diverse and mostly didn't know each other, but they were not from the mainstream of society. One participant was a man living in his car. Another was living in a shack that was painted with the words "God Saves" all over the front. There was a woman who had been the successful founder of a non-profit agency, until an earlier abuse began to show up in her dreams and unravel her life. Another woman had been beaten as a child, by her father, using a Bible; she felt physical revulsion when anyone promoted the Christian faith to her.

For their participation, each of these people were provided only with bus tokens for travel, and lunch on both days. Some of the people didn't stay for the whole meeting. Some were incapable of sitting and focusing for any length of time. Others balked at expressing themselves. Three left but returned later to watch from the back of the room.

The group wasn't an easy one to facilitate. Each had a story to tell and needed to be heard. But in the final analysis, they responded like anyone else. They looked at the issue sincerely and reached a clear and powerful consensus. They all agreed that they wanted to be self-sufficient. But they also said to mainstream America, "We are different from you. We are damaged in some way that you find hard to understand and accept. The welfare system you've designed is well suited to helping mainstream people get back on their feet, but it does not serve us. In fact, it does the opposite—it holds us down. We need a different kind of help, provided by people who understand this." Once determining this, they spontaneously started planning other meetings to arrange better help for others like themselves.

The most important lesson from this weekend was that, even in a case where most all the people were suffering from post-traumatic stress disorder, chemical abuse, or immense stress in their lives, the group could achieve Choice-creating dialogue and reach wise consensus. The difficult facilitation challenge in this situation was to recognize that people were being hurt by statements that didn't seem hurtful. The woman who had been beaten with the Bible, for instance, couldn't be fully protected from the pain she suffered each time someone promoted his or her religious conviction to the group. But the overall result was that, even in this difficult setting, the process worked.

It's Your Turn

Obviously, experiments with Wisdom Councils are just now getting underway. If you "get" the potential of this approach, and particularly if you see how important the Citizens Amendment is, I suggest you help awaken other people to it by talking to them, and by proposing a Wisdom Council in your city, company, professional society, union, church, etc. With the help of author and consultant, Nancy Rosanoff, the town council of Pleasantville, N.Y. began one in the fall of 2001; the Department of Agriculture in Washington State is beginning one in 2002; and Wisdom Council committees are forming in a few large cities. (For more current information see The Center for Wise Democracy at www.wisedemocracy.org.)

Each time a Wisdom Council is adopted, everyone in the organization will grow in understanding about Choice-creating, the competence of ordinary people, knowledge about Wisdom Councils, and the potential benefits of the Citizens Amendment. They also grow in their understanding of particular issues, about personal empowerment, and in their capacity for change.

The suggested strategy is:

1) Talk with friends and neighbors about the concepts in this book. You might gather people for a series of meetings where each chapter of the book is a separate topic.

2) Contact your national and state representatives about the value of the Wisdom Council and the Citizens Amendment. Make sure they know about it, and that you support it.

3) Propose a Wisdom Council in the organizations and systems of which you are a part. For help, contact the Center for Wise Democratic Processes at their web site: www.wisedemocracy.org.

When you talk about this idea with others, you may encounter emotional resistance. That's understandable. The idea is quite safe, but it challenges some closely held assumptions about life that many of us hold dear—like the need to have someone or something be in charge, the supremacy of the rule of law, the idea that life is a competition, the elitist dogma that only special people are capable of leading, the reassuring idea that the Founders were better than we are, and the notion that change must be controlled.

The psychological discomfort of challenging these ideas is nothing in comparison to the risk we face by not going ahead with the Citizens Amendment. Key to helping people overcome their resistance to it is to help them remember an issue they care about deeply, one that is particularly important to them. It's why I led off this book with the question, "What is fundamentally the most important issue we face as a society?" Once they identify a high-care issue and realize that there is little hope of resolving it in the present system, they naturally become more open to new ideas. In the end, this idea is not just a "nice to have," or some interesting improvement to our system. It is essential. *We must transform our system so that it becomes sustainable.* The Amendment offers us a way to do this and more—to make our lives and our children's lives safer, more productive, and more fulfilling.

— C —

How to Make a Decision Without Really Making a Decision

By Tom Atlee

When I first saw a decision being made without any decision-making I was trapped with hundreds of my fellow community members in a fertilizer factory in Western Colorado. The place stank like anything, and it was stifling hot. The towering sheet-metal roof was bellowing with thousands of gallons of water smashing down on it from an unstoppable herd of thunderclouds charging by thousands of feet above us. Jostling together in our sopping rain gear, we were not happy campers.

Four hundred people from all walks of life were trying to live together in a tent city that moved 15 miles down the road every day or two. We joked that our lives were "in-tents." We were the 1986 cross-country Great Peace March for Global Nuclear Disarmament and we were getting ready to fall apart. (We'd already fallen apart once when our sponsoring organization, Pro-Peace, went bankrupt and stranded all 1200 of us in the California desert. Eight-hundred of us went home. The 400 of us trapped in the fertilizer factory were the ones who'd finally gotten rolling again after two weeks holed up on a Barstow MX track back in March looking for new support and leadership. But that's a whole 'nother story!)

At any rate, here it was June already and we were being eaten away from the inside by a conflict that just wouldn't stop: the familiar war between "maintaining an acceptable appearance for the rest of the world" and "expressing our authentic selves." Nearly every community has its own version of this. Ours had been festering for almost two months before we landed in the fertilizer factory (we'd been setting up on its lawn when the storm rolled in). Our two polarized factions were: "We should march along in orderly rows to impress the media and maintain order in the face of traffic!" and "We should move at our own pace in a strung-out line so we can appreciate the natural world and chat with people in homes and schools we pass!" You can pretty much imagine who was on each side. And each side was ready to leave the march "if you people are going to wreck the march like that!"

But today we were momentarily drawn together by our common enemy, the rain. Taking advantage of our temporary communion, a few wise marchers set up a portable speaker system right there amidst the piles of odiferous chemicals, suggesting that anyone who wished to should take a two-minute turn speaking into the microphone about our conflict. So we did that, with great passion and messiness.

"How can we talk about peace and then force everyone to march like a military unit?!!"

"How do you expect to get disarmament if the media can make fun of us as a raggle-taggle mob of hippies?!!"

"How do we expect to get to Washington if we can't get along?!!"

"No one has a right to dictate to me how I walk!"

"Someone's going to get hit by an upset motorist in some city if we don't get some discipline around here."

"I get all my energy from the sky and the trees. If I'm too crowded with other people I lose touch with that."

"Hey, folks, we're all in this together. We're just like the Russians and the Americans. We have to learn to resolve our conflicts peacefully."

It went on like that for two hours, with each person speaking only once. As it proceeded, I noticed that speakers were increasingly

252

taking into account what previous people had said. Even though there was no back-and-forth, and no facilitator, the monologues began to sound more and more like dialogue. I was really blown away when one speaker after another began saying things that had only occurred to me moments before. I heard the ambivalences and nuances in my own head and heart being spoken and wrestled with in the public conversation I was part of. I started to sense us all working our way into what some native peoples call "One Big Mind." From the inside, I could feel that big Peace March Mind struggling to come to terms with all the elements of this difficult problem that it faced. It was doing just what my own mind does: "Well, let's see, if I do this, then ... but no, that wouldn't be so good. So I should try this, and then ... But I need to take into account this other thing ... etc."

And then someone said: "Why don't we all walk together in the cities and let people walk at their own pace in the country?" The next person said, "Well, I was going to talk about my experience as a media photographer, and the sorts of shots we like, and I was sort of thinking it would be good to be all together with the flags up front, but then I realized this new suggestion seems best of all. High shots of the march strung out along a country road, plus talking to farmers and all that would be great—but you'd need to be massed together for a city shot to make sense." And the next person said, "Well, we could just call it city mode and country mode and just do it." And then the rain stopped. After two hours of unremitting clatter, the silence was deafening. Without further comment, we streamed out into the dusk to finish putting up our tents.

As I stepped out into the flooded fields I suddenly realized that no decision had been made. No motion was made. No vote was taken. No one checked for consensus. Nothing was announced or recorded. The group just "knew" how we were going to behave as we marched down the streets and highways of America. And, in subsequent months, the overwhelming majority of us did just that.

Years later I read that Oren Lyons, faith-keeper of the Turtle Clan of the Onandaga Iroquois, said of his tribal council tradition: "We just keep talking until there's nothing left but the obvious truth." Once "the obvious truth" has been found, there is no need for a "decision." Such truth not only sets people free—it allows a group or community to self-organize.

The word "decision" derives from Latin words meaning "to cut away." It comes from the same root as "incision"—"to cut in." To decide is to cut away all the other alternatives but one. If you are considering options 1-6, a decision picks option 4 and cuts away options 1, 2, 3, 5 and 6 (to say nothing of 7-419!). When people "hammer out a compromise," there's even more cutting going on—a cutting and pasting of trade-offs. And "forging an agreement" requires a lot of heat and even more hammering.

In contrast, what happened in that Colorado fertilizer factory in the summer of 1986 was more like a group realization (a collective "a-ha!" experience) or a seed sprouting. No cutting, no hammering, nothing being pasted together or traded-off—just a set of conditions that helped the obvious truth emerge. Instead of slicing, pounding and constructing, the energy was more like emergence, sprouting, bubbling up, being born, breaking through.

Of course the breakthrough came after a lot of turbulent hoo-hah about all the aspects of the issue, all the feelings, all the stories people were telling themselves and each other, all the information connected to this or that possibility. I've come to think of this as the necessary cultivation of the Earth in preparation for planting, or like making compost, or like midwifing a birth. This is "setting the conditions" needed to help the natural, obvious truth emerge—that bigger truth that takes into account all the different pieces of the puzzle. The struggly, juicy work early on provides the nutrient base for the ultimate discovery of that big truth.

I believe there are at least five requirements for powerful "non-decision-making," and for discovering big obvious truths:

1) Diversity: Without diversity, there is no creative tension, and little chance of seeing a bigger picture. Any group has lots of diversity, but sometimes the right kind of diversity is needed. Consultant Meg Wheatley offers a great question that can be asked over and over: "Who else should be in this conversation?" But diversity needs help to avoid bogging down in argumentation so it can discover its true resource-full-ness.

2) Passion: Without passion there is no energy to drive discovery. Too often we are urged to be "dispassionate" because passion is so often associated with dogmatism and inflexibility. But passion is where the creative juice is, where the caring is, where everything that is truly important lives. Passion helps us break out of fixed ideas and preconceptions long enough to become aligned with the passions of other people. This generates the power needed to realize shared visions and solutions.

3) Motivation: Without commitment (or responsibility or necessity) there is nothing to keep people together in the conversation long enough to make it through the inevitable dissonance one encounters en route to the shared excitement of creative discovery. The emergence of true breakthroughs is seldom neat and pretty. All creativity is messy and some is fun. But if we're going to get through the messy parts, we have to hang in there. (This is a secret probably every communitarian reluctantly knows.)

4) Deep Dialogue: By "deep dialogue" I mean exploration towards shared understanding, connection and possibility. Deep dialogue isn't a method. It is a quality of inquiry and conversation characterized by interest, listening and respect. It can be achieved by agreement, by group culture, by practice, by accident or by facilitation. In our Peace March for example, we had already developed a group culture of "talking stick circles"—the native American practice of passing an object around a circle, with each person who holds it "speaking the truth from their heart." We'd practiced doing circles for several months, and that spirit helped generate the deep dialogue that resulted when our "talking stick" was a microphone.

5) Enough Time: How much time is "enough time"? Sometimes it is ten minutes. Sometimes it is ten months. Often "enough time" includes leaving an issue to lie fallow—letting it be gnawed at by people between meetings, letting perspectives and situations shift incrementally—before coming back to it again. Enough is enough. And those communities that acknowledge the power of ripeness and the essential continuity of community conversation—and therefore help their shared understandings develop "in their own good time"—reap the richest harvests.

Just as good cultivation or midwifery doesn't guarantee a great harvest or a healthy baby, good group process doesn't guarantee the emergence of Greater Truth. However, we'll only be able to evoke shared insight with any frequency if we use good processes well.

Choice-creating process was created by consultant Jim Rough of Port Townsend, Washington (see www.ToBE.net for information and training opportunities). It is the centerpiece of a practice called "Dynamic Facilitation" which encourages people and ideas to change as a conversation unfolds. Anything done to help such transformational conversation happen qualifies as Dynamic Facilitation. Jim contrasts "transformational talking" with "transactional talking" or discussion. Transactional talking is when unchanging people bat solid ideas back and forth like a Ping-Pong ball. "Discussion" derives from the same root as "percussion"—a root meaning "to hit." In contrast, transformational talking is more flowing and exploratory.

The Choice-creating process works best where a group faces a thorny shared problem they all care about. The Dynamic Facilitator writes what they say up on four chart pad pages, labeled:

- Problem Statements (or Situation Statements or Inquiries)
- Solutions (or Possibilities or Options)
- Concerns
- Data

Most processes try to get clear on the problem first, then discuss it, then figure out a solution, etc. Choice-creating process just plucks these things like fruit as they arise from the ongoing conversation, with no effort to organize them.

The group usually starts with some problem statement which evokes people's suggestions about how to handle it. Most familiar processes treat suggestions as proposals. But in Choice-creating each suggestion is just written on the Solutions page.

Furthermore, at any point someone may say, "Wait a minute. We're barking up the wrong tree. There's actually a much deeper (or broader or other) problem here ..." The facilitator writes their new problem statement on the Problems page and—if the group is interested in it—follows their energy. There's no effort to hold the conversation to any linear train of thought.

If someone says, "That's absurd! That would distract us from our basic mission here!" the facilitator writes that down on the Concerns sheet, nipping conflict in the bud while noting each person's contribution. If someone says, "We're forgetting there are thousands of people in this town who are not part of our community who are also interested in this issue," that's just written on the Data sheet.

The facilitator lets people know they've been heard and keeps the conversation moving forward. He or she doesn't revise what's already written, or check whether a piece of Data is factual or not, or try to get the group to pick the best solution from those listed. Whatever is said is logged on the big sheets in front of the room.

Sometimes the facilitator will dig a bit, trying to put some meat on the bones. For example, if someone says, "The real problem is X!" the facilitator might write that down and say, "You're saying that the real problem is X. Is that right? OK. So let's say you're king of the world. How would you handle X?"—and writes down the answer on the Solutions page. "And you over there. What do you think?"

In the early stages of the Choice-creating process people tend to share things they already knew when they walked in: their sense of the problem, their ideas about what should be done, their concerns and information. This is exactly what should happen, and the facilitator helps it along. All those pieces of the puzzle need to be out in the group space. And participants need to feel heard, to free their attention to hear and creatively interact with each other.

A well-facilitated Choice-creating process will usually evoke breakthroughs if: a) all the participants are really interested in solving the problem or breaking through on the topic; b) the group of participants is consistent over time; and c) there is enough time available, preferably several meetings, each several hours long.

Choice-creating works best with a facilitator trained in the Dynamic Facilitation process. Smart organizations and communities will share facilitators so that every member of each group can participate in that group's meetings and the facilitator has no special interest in the outcome.

Other useful Big Truth processes include:

• Listening Circles. An object is passed around the circle of participants. Each consecutive holder of the object speaks from their heart. No facilitator is needed.

• Fishbowl. In a group conflict, members of Side A converse in a central circle while others watch. Then Side B converses while others watch. Then other sides or no-sides take their turns. The whole sequence repeats two or more times. Facilitation is often useful.

• World Cafe. The group breaks up into subgroups who talk for a while and then mix randomly into other subgroups and continue talking, ultimately returning to their original subgroup. Someone needs to ring a bell to signal shifts.

• Open Space Conferences. Participants who are passionate about a given topic create their own sessions on aspects of that topic. Active facilitation is needed at the beginning.

• Consensus Process. Explore a topic and options until all agree on the best approach. Usually consensus is a decision-making process, but sometimes the emergent solution is so clear that "deciding" is a formality. Facilitation is advisable.

Tom Atlee is founder of *Innovations in Democracy*, (www.democracyinnovation.org), a project of The Co-Intelligence Institute in Eugene, Oregon.

(This article is reprinted with permission from *Communities* magazine, <fic.ic.org/cmag> or 800-462-8240.)

Society's Breakthrough!

Acknowledgments

Thank you to the many people who have trusted and supported me while developing the ideas in this book—especially Jean Rough, Don Miller, Tom Atlee, Michelle Hensel, DeAnna Martin, Rosa Zubizarreta, Dan Rough, Bonnie Yocum, Adin Rogovin, Paul Bauck, Caspar Davis, Zoe Calder, Elliot Shuford, Tracee Parker, Rima Phillips, Dave Kratzer, George Lindamood, Bill Shephard, Kerry Bourke, Gus Jaccaci, Jeff Hatfield, Yvonne Jarosz, George Beahm, Ned Crosby, Pat Benn, Pennie Stasik O'Grady, Marilyn Norris, Nylah Chilton, Jim Kirk, Roger Cramer, Dave Newlin, Nancy Wilson, Allen Frank, Grant Dunlap, John Moriarty Karen Valdes, Chip Shelton, Robert L. Powers, Tom Cronin, Tim Kaufman-Osborn, Paul Everett, Stan Figgins, Tom Bender, Don Straus, the participants in my Dynamic Facilitation Skills seminars, and workers at the Korbel sawmill from 1980-1984.

Also, thank you to people and organizations that have taught me about creative thinking and transformation—especially: the founders and volunteers at the Guild for Psychological Studies, including Elizabeth B. Howes, Madeline McMurray, and David McMurray; the Creative Initiative Foundation, including Harry and Emilia Rathbun; Creative Problem Solving Institutes, including Sid Parnes, Bill Idol, George Land, and Oz Swallow; and to Russell A. Lockhart, Jungian Analyst.

LaVergne, TN USA
16 September 2009
158046LV00002B/2/A